The 20th anniversary edition
of the pioneering ADR book in Canada

IN THIS EDITION

THE DEFINITIVE HISTORY OF THE ADR MOVEMENT!

As I predicted in 1989, this book has indeed been an invaluable reference on Alternative Dispute Resolution. It is as relevant today as ever, and in light of the remarkable developments in ADR since its publication, we can now appreciate how visionary these ideas were in 1989. This book and its sequel have much to tell us about resolving conflict.

—The Hon. Allen Linden, former Justice of the Federal Court of Appeal (Canada)

PRAISE FOR
ALTERNATIVE DISPUTE RESOLUTION THAT WORKS!

Experience with ADR in the United States has resulted in many benefits…I commend this book to anyone interested in the people's access to justice.

—Frank Evans, Chief Justice, First Judicial District Court of Appeals, Texas

I can testify to the effectiveness of mediation as the most effective tool in the resolution of labour conflict…Ernie Tannis has demonstrated in this book that the same principle and process can be applied wherever conflicts exist.

—W.P. (Bill) Kelly, former Associate Deputy Minister of Labour, Canada

We must find ways, therefore, to resolve our disputes more efficiently and less expensively. Ernest Tannis…has assembled for us much helpful material pointing in the direction we must follow. We would do well to follow.

—Mr. Justice Allen Linden, President, Law Reform Commission of Canada

With his penetrating and insightful overview of the ADR revolution, Ernie Tannis effectively demonstrates…better ways to resolve disputes….

—Brian S. Mandell, Ph.D., Professor of International Affairs, Carleton University

Mr. Tannis' remarkable enthusiasm for ADR will expedite that process.

—Justice T. David Marshall, Executive Director, Canadian Judicial Centre

Constructive dispute resolution demands creative solutions…Ernie Tannis provides a succinct and insightful overview of options available. It should be read by all problem solvers.

—Julien Payne, Q.C., LL.D., Professor of Common Law, University of Ottawa

…an insightful resource compendium on this increasingly vital subject, with valuable references to the Canadian, American, and international scenes.

—Frank E.A. Sander, Professor of Law,
Harvard Law School, Chairman, ADR Committee, American Bar Association

ALTERNATIVE DISPUTE RESOLUTION THAT WORKS!

A Note About the Cover Illustration

How do bouncing balls relate to ADR?

Small rubber balls proved to be an effective ice breaker for a group of youths during my opening remarks to a four-day conference on youth conflict resolution in Ottawa in 2007. Balls were thrown out to each of the 80 young participants from across Canada, producing laughter and an energetic discussion. To my pleasant surprise, later that week when the 40 adult chaperones arrived for my second keynote address, they asked for balls also! The balls created a connection between all the participants and demonstrated a symbolic ADR principle: even when we have differences, we can always find practical tools to help us interact—and we shouldn't forget to have fun too.

For more details on the bouncing balls story, please visit www.adrcentre.org.

To see the materials from the youth conflict resolution conference, please visit www.ethnocultural.ca.

A Note About the Back Cover Sculpture, *Justice?*

Sculpted by John Tappin, completed in 1986
Commissioned by Ernest G. Tannis, 1981

To me, this piece depicts the body of jurisprudence seeking to be perfect and beautiful, with arms outstretched to reach out to people and provide access to justice. One hand bears the iron fist of the law while the other is a hand of mercy.

The sculpture is headless because unless people have an opportunity to fully *speak*, actively *listen* to one another, and really *see* others' points of view and perceptions, then justice is not only blind but can also become deaf and dumb, incapable of thought or imagination.

ALTERNATIVE DISPUTE RESOLUTION THAT WORKS!

SECOND EDITION

Ernest G. Tannis
B.A., J.D., C. Med., Acc. FM (OAFM)
Solicitor, Mediator, Ontario Notary Public, Negotiation Consultant,
Member of the Law Society of Upper Canada

Published by the ADR Centre (Canada) Inc.

© Ernest G. Tannis
ISBN 978-0-9813864-0-9

Published in Canada by Ernest G. Tannis
Legal deposit 2010
Library and Archives Canada

Printed in Canada

Front cover: Photos.com
Back cover: sculpture by John Tappin, photos by Joseph Nassif

Library and Archives Canada Cataloguing in Publication

Tannis, Ernest G., 1948-
Alternative dispute resolution that works / Ernest G. Tannis. -- 2nd ed.

Includes bibliographical references.
ISBN 978-0-9813864-0-9

1. Dispute resolution (Law)--Canada. I. Title.

KE8615.T35 2010   347.71'09   C2010-903868-1
KF9084.T35 2010

DEDICATION

Dedicated to those from whose efforts this book evolved, and to those whom we all love—our children. For me this gift is cherished with my daughter, Chanda; son, Derek; nephew, Rick; and step-daughter, Kim; and to the person without whose trust and support over the years it would never have appeared, my wife, Mary. —*1989*

For the subject of our argument is no trifling matter. It is the question of the right manner of life.

—Plato, *Republic*

An invasion of armies can be resisted, but not an idea whose time has come.

—Victor Hugo

It takes two to speak the truth—one to speak and one to hear.

—Henry David Thoreau

CONTENTS

PREFACE TO THE SECOND EDITION

Do not go where the path may lead, go instead where there is no path and leave a trail.
—Ralph Waldo Emerson

On reflection, this quote expresses what I have felt lately when recollecting events since the original edition of this book was released in June 1989. At that time, it was the first book on Alternative Dispute Resolution (ADR) to appear in Canada, thanks to a courageous publisher, Randy Hoffman of Captus Press at York University Campus in Toronto.

As I have said many times since then, I never set out to write a book; rather, it emerged from a paper on ADR that I presented in 1988 to lawyers, judges, the Ontario Attorney General and those in the administration of justice. I didn't know it at the time, but many involved in conflict resolution said the paper accurately reflected the current state of ADR, and began circulating it around the world. In fact, one lawyer actually filed the paper in Court and requested the Court take "judicial notice" of ADR (meaning the Court would accept ADR as an obvious or notorious fact without the need for further evidence). I never considered publishing the paper until that was suggested by Neil Sargent, the chairman of the Carleton University law faculty, where I was teaching a course. As the saying goes, the rest is history; the book took on a life of its own and I simply followed along.

I have always considered my ADR journey a personal search for healing; a journey that was inspired many years ago by my urge to find better ways of resolving disagreements. It was 1985, and at the time I was dismayed at the inadequacies of the legal system and saddened by the civil war in Lebanon— my father's ancestral home—and how it was hurting children. I wanted to help the situation from afar, but how? When I embarked on this unplanned journey I soon learned that we will go far with ADR!

I am now inclined to believe that the book's publication in 1989 was not simply an accident or aberration. The year 1989 is now widely regarded as a watershed year in our recent history; in fact, the editors of *TIME* magazine commemorated the significance of that year in a 2009 book aptly titled *1989: The Year That Defined Today's World: From Berlin to Beijing, from* The Simpsons *to* Exxon Valdez. The year marked the convergence of several threshold events: The Cold War came to an end with the signing of the first Arms Control Treaty between the U.S.A. and Russia, and the World Wide Web found its genesis in a paper by Timothy Berners-Lee describing a global project that, ironically, would build on military technology to allow people to work together and share information by combining their knowledge in a web of hypertext documents. In retrospect, these two developments in world affairs toward reconciliation and information sharing unconsciously formed a backdrop for the gathering of those ideas that evolved into the original book, *Alternative Dispute Resolution That Works!*

Perhaps it is a metaphor for the times that the World Wide Web and ADR movements have continued to expand exponentially together and will continue to go forward hand in hand in developments yet to come. This speaks well for **A D**ignified **R**esolution (a description that I think better characterizes the essence of ADR) to become an increasingly preferred way for how we treat one another. Surely we need to be more self-aware to change our attitudes and practices, and we can begin by rephrasing how we speak to one another. For example, rather than say 'kill two birds with one stone,' why not say 'feed two birds in one nest'?

As the twentieth anniversary of this book was approaching in 2009, I was encouraged by many to have the original book edited and reprinted, and the result is this second edition. Although the text has been edited the content has not been updated, except for a few specific examples that I have footnoted. In Chapter 1, for example, I include a couple of footnotes to help piece together what I believe is the definitive history of the ADR movement. I trust that this second edition is received in the spirit in which it has been prepared—as a contribution to the ever-deepening and ever-widening discussion on ADR, which Derek Bok, Harvard Law School president, many years ago called "the center of one of the most creative social experiments of our time."

In conjunction with the publication of this second edition, the second book in the ADR series has also been published and released. Titled *Alternative Dispute Resolution At Work: 18 universal truths that I have learned about ADR*, the second book summarizes what I have gleaned over the decades from interacting with individuals and institutions, locally, nationally, and internationally.

Next year, I hope to complete the ADR trilogy with a third book, as yet untitled, that will explore the breadth and depth of the ADR field through a retrospective of the five-year run of the weekly Alternative Dispute Resolution radio program that I co-hosted with Gary Michaels on CHIN radio in Ottawa. The program began on February 4, 2005 with a show on trust and ended almost exactly five years later, on February 1, 2010, with a discussion of the book *Peace Guerilla* by Ben Hoffman and ADR's future international scope. In between, we hosted 260 shows and talked to 1,500 guests, and the program won two awards from the Canadian Ethnic Media Association in 2007 and 2008.

There remains a kind of mystery in treading into new and unknown territory, as many brave explorers in history will attest. But what is no longer a mystery is that the projections and predictions of numerous thinkers and doers, many of which were captured in the original book, have actually come true throughout societies all over the globe. Many are building on the teachings and practices from centuries-old traditions, and on the art of diplomacy.

When one compares the state of ADR twenty years ago with the situation today, it becomes obvious that this ADR movement is in fact "a trend emerging from the bottom up and not a fad coming from the top down," as I wrote in the original introduction.

Inspired by a comment from Brenda Quinn, who so ably edited this second edition and intellectually prodded me on the content, I was challenged to focus on other specific changes over the past two decades, and when I actually investigated these developments I was inspired and encouraged to realize how far we have come. Here are few of the many developments in ADR since 1989:

ADR education and training

In 1989 there were few academically and school-based programs and curricula, but today hundreds of post-secondary institutions and law schools in dozens of countries teach ADR and conflict resolution. Upon admission to the bar, more lawyers are being taught about the importance of learning and applying ADR in their cases where appropriate. As the ADR field matures, credentials and accreditations with various ADR organizations are being proffered to the public, which is resulting in an increasing number of service providers everywhere.

ADR applications

In the courts: The courts are now enforcing arbitration agreements and arbitrator decisions and supporting mediations. Jurists are taking a leadership role in integrating ADR into the fabric of the Rule of Law.

In business and trade: ADR has been formalized in many pieces of legislation, indicating that mediation and arbitration are often mandatory and not just voluntary. ADR clauses are increasingly finding their way into domestic contracts, and particularly into international contracts, due to the varying jurisdictions in global disputes. We should also be mindful that international negotiation is accomplished through treaties. ADR is now a well-established part of the worldwide dispute resolution system; for example, global sites such as Wikipedia and eBay have mediation and arbitration mechanisms available.

In everyday situations: I have always considered ADR to be an everyday life skill and it seems that society has begun to accept it as such. Mediation processes, for example, are now increasingly used in schoolyards, in consumer transactions, and in many other aspects of life.

ADR information

Twenty years ago there were relatively few publications or gatherings on ADR. Today, we have a plethora of journals, newsletters, books and conferences—and millions of references on the internet—on various ADR subjects, including conflict resolution, mediation, arbitration and negotiation.

All of these advancements, and many more that are yet to come, provide more suitable processes for those who want more non-adversarial options for problem-solving. And there also needs to be some sort of post-confrontation mechanism that would allow us to address common issues in a co-operative way, learn from past adversarial relationships, and find the deep-rooted causes of the confrontation that could set the stage for future disputes. We all subscribe to fire prevention, and health and dental management to avoid damage and pain, so why not apply the same protocols to conflict prevention?

Around the world we can all work to promote ADR by implementing the idea for UNICRY (UNiversal International Conflict Resolution Years). Originally an acronym for the proposed United Nations International Conflict Resolution Year, UNICRY instead became a global, citizen-based movement at the suggestion of my colleague Jeremy Wright, an economist who until his passing in 2009 dedicated his life to an ethical, fair financial system as a basis for resolving world problems. I discuss UNICRY in Chapter 9, and make several suggestions on how it could be implemented practically in our communities. Through UNICRY and through other means, it is ultimately up to all of us to find ways to reduce the human and economic costs of conflicts.

I have believed for some time that if we could merge our urge to protect the environment with our urge to find non-violent solutions, the result would be like combining ADR with nature. In other words, we would then be able to look not just at the forest of human issues but also at the trees of each person's life. That would naturally lead us more closely to the harmony for which everyone strives. My friend David Farrell, who passed away in 2004, was well known for his reminders that in our world, we have a *Legal System* and not a *Justice System*. David was more aware of that reality than most, given his long career at the Department of Justice and a retirement dedicated to Restorative Justice. Our search for justice is essentially "just us." This eventually requires that we all more fully appreciate and apply the art of listening.

I hope that this 20th anniversary edition is yet another way to broadcast the rising chorus of voices that have united in the quest for conflict resolution, prevention and management—a chorus that can now be clearly heard above the din of violence and disputes that rage in our own homes, neighbourhoods and in our extended human family. We are all neighbours on this planet, and therefore we should point the way, not a finger.

In real life there must be a balance between the fist and the handshake, depicted in the *Justice?* sculpture that now appears on the back of this second edition. U.S. President Barack Obama put it this way in his 2009 inaugural address: "We will extend a hand if you are willing to unclench your fist." We have choices; let us choose wisely, not poorly. What legacy will we leave to the next generations? Isn't it better to be able to say: We tried to find a better way?

For me personally, this movement is summed up in a plain phrase that came to me near the beginning of my ADR trek that began in earnest in 1985: "World peace through inner peace."

May each of us find that plane of inner peace on a chaotic planet.

Ernest G. Tannis
Ottawa, Ontario, Canada
September 2010

For continuing updates on ADR please visit www.adrcentre.org.
Contact the author at ernestgtannis@adrcentre.org

ACKNOWLEDGEMENTS

In which, if I have in any point receded from that which is commonly received,
it hath been with a purpose of proceeding in melius [to something better]
and not in aliud [to something new].
—Sir Francis Bacon, *Advancement of Learning*

I would like to extend my deepest thanks to the publishing team responsible for this second edition—facilitator Robbi Hay, editor Brenda Quinn, and designer Miriam Bloom—for their encouragement and prodding to ensure that this second edition was completed. Unlike the original book that evolved on its own, this second edition was intentional. Although it was my first experience in publishing, their collective expertise, guidance and patience were instrumental in allowing this book to emerge, and in giving me the inspiration and foundation to move on to complete the sequel book. Also, I wish to thank my colleague, Esther Van Gennip, for her profound support, and my daughter, Chanda (who finally read the original book!) for her valuable insights. *—September 2010*

It is a privilege for me to present findings and share thoughts about Alternative Dispute Resolution (ADR); for the opportunity to do so, I must acknowledge the vast support of a small army of people at all tiers of society who have generously given of their time, advice and resources in many ways over the past two years. Many pages would be needed to list the hundreds of people who have helped, lent their names, or been otherwise involved with the project since the summer of 1986, including the youths, parents, business people, politicians, journalists, lawyers, judges, police officers, educators at all levels, and those in theatre and the other arts.

Contacts in Canada, the United States, Australia and Europe have given us access to extensive literature about ADR, and more important, have helped to locate dedicated and talented individuals knowledgeable about the subject and its history. I thank them for this.

Thanks are due to the staff, officers, board members and governors of the Dispute Resolution Centre for Ottawa-Carleton (DRCCOC) and the Canadian Institute of Conflict Resolution (CICR), who form part of that core of people that continue to meet the challenges and demands of creating and maintaining socially useful organizations.

In particular, I wish to express my profound gratitude to the following members of the bench and bar, whose encouragement and contributions have been more instrumental than they would admit:

Michael Andrews, Earl Atnikov, Sen. Jean Bazin, Judge Paul Belanger, John M. Bergin, Andrejs Berzins, Richard Bosada, Norman Bowley, Lloyd Brennan, Michael Cochrane, Hon. David Daubney, Maria de Souza, Jacques Emond, Paul Emond, Judge Frank Evans, David Farrell,* Don Fraser, John Goodwin, Lawrence Greenspon, Doug Grenkie, Gordon Henderson,* Rt. Hon. Raymon Hnatyshyn,* Prue Kestner, Clarke W. Lackert, Walter Langley, Mr. Justice Allen Linden, Leonard Max, Terry McCarthy, Donald McRae, Mr. Justice Gerald Morin, Orm Murphy, Robert Nelson, Julien Payne, Pat Peacock, William Rankin, Larry Ray, William Riley, Evita Roche, Margaret Ross, Neil Sargent, Hon. Ian Scott,* Bill Simpson, Jim Vilvang, Jeremy Wright,* Maurice Wright,* Professor Douglas Wurtele,* and members of the ADR Committee of the American Bar Association (ABA).

For their assistance in the various aspects of preparing this manuscript, I must also thank Nicole Brown, Nadine Faulkner, Y.A. George Hynna, and Randy Hoffman and the entire staff of Captus Press.

Many thanks to my family, who helped me in every way, particularly my magnificent relatives at Tannis Food Distributors and my brother, Ralph, whose support to date has been instrumental in my ADR journey.

Ernest G. Tannis
Ottawa, Ontario
June 1989

The author wishes to acknowledge and thank the following organizations and individuals for permission to reprint articles and excerpts:

American Bar Association, Special Committee on Dispute Resolution

Canadian Bar Association

Canadian Bar Association, Ontario Continuing Legal Education

Center for Public Resources, Inc.

Church Council on Justice and Corrections

Education and Law Project, Simon Fraser University and Pat Pitsula

Judge Frank Evans, First Court of Appeals, Houston, Texas

National Institute for Dispute Resolution (NIDR)

---

* passed away since 1989

National Association Active in Criminal Justice (NAACJ)

Russell L. Horrocks

International Young Lawyers Association (Association internationale des jeunes avocats, AIJA)

John S. Kelly

Law Reform Commission of Canada and Andrew Pirie

Queen's Printer and Ministry of Attorney General, Province of British Columbia

Queen's Printer, Province of Ontario

Frank E.A. Sander, Stephen B. Goldberg, Eric D. Green, and Little Brown & Co.

Travelers Insurance (The Connecticut ADR Project Inc.)

FOREWORD

We are in an age of transition. Old and new institutions are being critically examined to determine if they meet the dynamics of a rapidly changing and shrinking world. Time and space are being annihilated by the computer and new means of travel and communication.

The time-honoured methods of conflict resolution and conflict management are subject to challenge and demand restructuring to meet the needs of the times. The adversary system and the Court structure as traditionally known to us are under pressure for change and streamlining.

In terms of conflict resolution, new techniques are commanding increasing attention. The increasing cost of litigation and the delays inherent in the Court system have resulted in a growing interest in methods of resolving disputes outside the traditional Court structure.

Historically, settlements have saved the Courts from overcrowding and delays. New legal relationships and new laws arising from them have led to many situations where resolution by settlement has become difficult, if not impossible. The Charter, environmental issues, human rights legislation, the right to privacy, access to information, and the new *Family Law Act* are but a few of such new legal problems. Legal aid inhibits settlements because it minimizes the risk as to costs. We must find ways to relieve this congestion. Alternative dispute mechanism is one option. It also enables the public to participate in the system. Elitism has long been a criticism of the Courts and the legal profession.

However, apart from the limited area of labour disputes and to some extent family disputes, the dispute resolution techniques of mediation and arbitration have been slow to have gained the recognition in North America that they have enjoyed in Europe. In commercial disputes, the parties still tend to prefer to take the dispute to Court and to accept the trauma that goes with the "adversary system" and the attitude of confrontation that is inherent in it. In recent years, there has been a growing acceptance of the role that can be played by way of mediation and arbitration. In the fast-moving industrial/commercial world of the 1990s, business people cannot afford the luxury, and indeed the expense, that goes with the traditional trial procedure. Immediate resolution of problems saves not only time and expense but also the lasting wounds that are inherent in confrontation of a courtroom experience.

The former Chief Justice of the United States, Chief Justice Burger, as long ago as June 1976 expressed the need to examine arbitration as a technique for dispute resolution as follows:

> As the work of the courts increases, delays and costs will rise and the well-developed forms of arbitration should have wider use; lawyers, judges and social scientists of other countries cannot understand our failure to make greater use of the arbitration process to settle disputes.

Arbitration has had a long history. It is recorded that the Laws of Judges in the Code of Hebrew Law imposed a duty on a judge to ask the litigants at the outset of a case whether they wished to submit to arbitration to resolve the dispute. Arbitration was recognized as a method of dispute resolution in 1601 in the first statute relating to insurance. Arbitration acts are found in every county in England.

In the commercial field, business men are gaining confidence in mediation and arbitration as dispute resolution techniques. That confidence is growing because of the improved knowledge applicable to those techniques amongst those business men and the legal profession.

It is in the light of that background that the work of Ernest Tannis, *Alternative Dispute Resolution That Works!* must be assessed. His work is a welcome contribution to the literature of the law relating to a timely legal subject. His work reflects his dedication to the proposition that where there is a need someone must do something about it. Mr. Tannis has a reputation as a champion of good causes. His comprehensive work reviews extensively what has been done in the field of alternative dispute resolution elsewhere and what can be achieved by its adoption. It is a ready reference work for anyone interested in further information on a subject of growing interest—to anyone concerned with our system of justice. Mr. Tannis' infectious enthusiasm for his thesis emerges clearly from his work. It cannot help but further the acceptance of mechanisms that will relieve a Court system of congestion and aid business people to get on with their purpose with a minimum of confrontation, where difference of opinion and recollection occur.

As Mr. Tannis has pointed out, the Honourable Mr. Justice Zuber in his 1987 *Report on the Ontario Courts Inquiry,* in his recommendation 118 recommended that "A voluntary arbitration mechanism should be built into the justice system." The work of Mr. Tannis will provide a valuable service toward attaining this purpose.

Gordon F. Henderson, C.C., Q.C., LL.D.
Gowling and Henderson
Ottawa, Ontario, Canada
1989

ALTERNATIVE DISPUTE RESOLUTION THAT WORKS!

INTRODUCTION

Fellow citizens, we cannot escape history.
—Abraham Lincoln, Address to Congress, 1862

ALTERNATIVE DISPUTE RESOLUTION (ADR) has been described as a social phenomenon and a movement whose profound impact on our social fabric is finally being appreciated. Massive changes are on the horizon; in some jurisdictions, extraordinary and intriguing developments are occurring at a rapid pace, and in others they are only beginning to be appreciated. But most students are beginning to accept that these events are a trend emerging from the bottom up and not a fad coming from the top down—and therefore are likely to be permanent and not a passing fancy.

These developments, in turn, are considered by many social scientists to be only one part of a major transformation taking place in all disciplines. For example, a recent edition of *Psychology Today* noted that for the first time psychology is seriously concentrating on positive elements of human nature rather than the negative. A recent newspaper article quotes psychiatrists to the effect that all people will have to learn to cope with fundamental challenges to all our social assumptions. It seems there is a movement toward the empowerment of the individual because of the growing realization that perhaps it is the last vestige of hope.

In relation to the question of "justice" and the resolution of disputes, many activities and experiments are surfacing. Lawyers, like everyone else, are being compelled to come to terms with the times. To paraphrase the famous words of a diplomat, those lawyers believed to be out of tune with certain realities risk being left behind. And as Oliver Wendell Holmes warned: "A blind man is not required to see at his peril." (*The Common Law*, 1881.)

I have included a bibliography that reveals exciting literature on improving techniques and skills to achieve settlement. A new text, *Getting Disputes Resolved—Designing Systems to Cut the Cost of Conflict*, by the renowned mediator and speaker William Ury in collaboration with others, includes an interesting analysis of how we approach problem solving and describes success stories. The text holds promise for dispute resolution system designers, a new profession in its infancy, and proposes skills that lawyers could add to their professional practice—a result of the contention by some that conflict resolution is the fastest expanding growth industry of our times.

Some of the literature is specifically for judges and lawyers. One book of particular relevance to the legal profession and the judiciary is *Effective Approaches to Settlement: A Handbook for Lawyers and Judges,* recently released by California Magistrate Wayne Brazil. Some of the judge's simple but essential principles are expanded in nuts-and-bolts detail, with considerations of the advantages of settlement over a trial process—control of cost, timing, procedure, information, privacy, flexible outcomes—and an examination of devices to resolve disputes—mediation, arbitration, case evaluation, mini-trials, and summary jury trials. The main part of the book deals with all aspects of the judicial settlement process, drawing upon hundreds of the judge's own experiences and a survey of more than 2,000 lawyers who support judicial intervention as mediators, in case or litigation management and in bridging the gap between the parties through judicially hosted settlement conferences or pretrials. Magistrate Brazil's principles include the following:

■ "To be a good lawyer it is essential to be good at settlement"
■ "Before proceeding, I should disclaim any notion that judges settle lawsuits. Clients and lawyers settle lawsuits"
■ "There are numerous ways a judge can improve the quality of settlement discussions."

Soon, no doubt, more Canadian-based literature will appear on dispute containment and settlement, and conflict resolution.

Hence, after almost two years of remarkably interesting research, networking, communications, program development, conferences, meetings, and reflection, I have been persuaded by both the inevitability and the promise of ADR, although I am still mindful of its limitations and deficiencies. Lawyers should see ADR as a challenge, not a threat.

In this book I present what can at best be called a condensation of some things that we have learned through our groups, and a few ideas that I have come to understand about ADR. The subject is so vast that I am reminded of Isaac Newton's response to the question of how one human being could know so much in a lifetime. Newton's reply: "I have but touched the seashore of the ocean of truth."

We probably all remember fellow students who were afraid to ask questions lest they be considered stupid. Yet a friend who is a teacher advises his students at the beginning of each year that the only stupid question is the one that is never asked. By asking we raise our awareness. I am reminded of Oliver Wendell Holmes' comment: "Man's mind, once stretched by a new idea, never regains its original dimensions."

Accordingly, this book is concerned with raising questions based on the dissemination of information. I have attempted to present as many relevant facts as possible, to set out some pertinent issues, and to describe some of the prevailing arguments about ADR from a list of sources. As a character said in Loggins' *The Just and the Unjust*:

> "...so we have to be careful, but I always remember you saying once that there was never any trouble with the law if you just keep your facts straight."

To some this information may be an eye-opener; to many it may be information to add to their current knowledge on the subject.

No one can or should try to rally the world to their side. As Mahatma Gandhi once said, "You must be the change you want to see in the world." It is my belief that lawyers are being challenged to change, to "retool" in the art of problem-solving to the extent, ironically, that change is in the nature of their domain and in their best interests. The potential is very exciting and the developments are quite exhilarating! I hope that you enjoy reading about these matters as expressed here.

In order to enhance readability, I include very few footnotes. Although this style is somewhat unorthodox it seemed to suit the type of narrative presented here. The lack of footnotes avoids regular distractions, for many sentences would contain a number of footnotes, and further, my point here is to tell a story not deliver a treatise; to impress upon you the facts, not impress you with apparatus.

Another reason for this method is the restriction of space. This book draws on the knowledge of a great number of people and includes notes from panel discussions, conferences, seminars, workshops and countless conversations with hundreds of people throughout the world. Many of these verbal exchanges would also have to be footnoted to give proper credit, which would become unwieldy. However, following the precedent set in a recent issue of the *Ontario Gazette* written by a Supreme Court Justice, in places I identify a quoted source generally, and at the end of the book provide a list of sources and references. This approach does have the distinct advantage of reducing the number of pages. I have a suspicion that I have not empirically studied, namely that the pulp and paper industry may be a wholly owned subsidiary of the legal profession!

Headlines are beginning to blare about ADR. We are becoming aware that the writing is on the wall, and that ADR is just around the corner. There is mounting evidence that the growing presence of ADR is having real and positive effects in virtually every area of human activity. Accordingly, I wish to seize this opportunity to provide as much information as I can, recognizing that this book can provide only a glimpse at the ADR sunrise and a suggested plan of action for our own community and society. The information and ideas presented here will be just one more contribution—and a useful contribution, I hope—to improve access to justice and to improve the quality of life for lawyers' clients, for lawyers themselves, and indeed, for others involved in their trusted tasks in the administration of justice.

Enthusiasm has been the hallmark of the two years' experience that gave rise to this book. It has been a fascinating, extraordinary and exciting journey. I hope that some of these emotions are imparted through these pages. However, as a practitioner, I know we are comfortable only when our observations, knowledge and beliefs can be translated into action. In that regard, I describe new ADR programs in the schools that are now in place, analyze details of existing ADR processes, and propose a new program called *Without Prejudice*, which would allow rank-and-file lawyers and ordinary business people to learn about, adopt and adapt ADR into their local communities. Perhaps we can all collaborate and develop an "ADR system that works."

It is excellent that conferences are taking place and studies are being done. The Canadian Bar Association has a committee under the able leadership of Bonita Thompson, Q.C., which will report at the mid-winter meeting in February 1989, in preparation for the annual meeting in the summer of 1989 when the committee will recommend how the CBA should proceed in the knowledge that ADR lies ahead. President Pat Peacock (who regards this issue as a priority), wrote a column in the October 1988 edition of the *National* titled "Alternative Dispute Resolution—CBA must encourage orderly development of this system." This is a wise approach.

I would like to make one general warning, though—and this is not aimed at anyone nor is it restricted to ADR—that the human tendency is to study, then monitor, then monitor who is monitoring, with the result that conferences become discussions only among those already involved. I understand that people resist change—and I appreciate that one tactic is to look busy—but, as the old adage says, after all is said and done, much is said and little is done. This is what management theorists call paralysis by analysis. Moreover, people involved could be tempted to create another set of professional credentials and institutions that will become just as complex and costly as the present legal system.

In the area of ADR, many agree with my concerns that this seems to be happening to some extent. Hence, is the time perhaps right to actually bring hands-on ADR programs and conflict skills workshops to society in a widespread way? The skills and precedents have been developed, and there are many people with expertise in all areas related to ADR who want to extend their services. In addition, there are sure to be a great number of others, including lawyers, who would want to volunteer time, pursue a career or add to their present repertory of skills in the area of dispute settlement and conflict resolution.

Yes, as we are often reminded, we must first crawl, then walk, and only then run. We also have to be on guard against the notion that we can control these developments. Things will evolve naturally as long as we allow people to participate in real-life programs and establish concrete processes; we must let people, including the professionals, take responsibility and have an opportunity to enhance their own life skills and professional livelihoods. We have to demystify ADR. There will be an orderly development only when we free ADR into natural development.

If we are urged, then let us be urgent (and organized). This is not about people taking the law into their own hands but into their own lives. This is not idealism, it is ideal; this is about us going beyond the mechanisms of the law with our prayer for relief, to grasp the meaning of the law with our plea for justice, to reach for mastery of the law with our petition for mercy.

What, then, is justice? Twenty years ago former Prime Minister Pierre Elliott Trudeau called for a "just" society in Canada. Only by delving into the etymology of the word "justice" can we gain direction on its meaning. According to the 1971 book, *An Aid to Bible Understanding*, the Hebrew meaning of justice is, "what is right in a fair and impartial way" and in accordance with a "standard" or "conveying the idea of a particular plan, custom, rule or procedure for doing things." Ultimately, justice is what is known as righteousness since "whereas justice has legal associations, basically there is no distinction between justice and righteousness." Or we can consult the Greek meaning of justice, which the book says is avenging or looking towards a judgement. "The proper exercise of justice by government authority likewise contributes to the happiness and well-being of its subjects."

In Chadman's *Cyclopedia of Law, Vol. 1*, the great English jurist Sir William Blackstone is quoted: "(God) has so intimately connected, so inseparably woven the laws of eternal justice with the happiness of each individual, that the latter cannot be attained but by observing the former; and, if the former be punctually obeyed, it cannot but induce the latter." Indeed, a former Chief Justice of the United States Supreme Court traced the source of our common law to the Ten Commandments. (But then, one is reminded of Malcolm Muggeridge's remark that the Ten Commandments are comparable to an examination paper: "…eight only to be attempted.")

Black's Law Dictionary, 4th edition, in the context of jurisprudence, cites case law to arrive at a definition of justice as "the constant and perpetual disposition to render every man his due" and includes the comments of John Bouvier (1787–1851) that "in the most extensive sense the word 'justice' differs little from 'virtue,' for it includes within itself the whole circle of virtues." Justice has also been described as "the crowning glory of virtues" (Cicero), "the great standing policy of civil society" (Edmund Burke), and "truth in action" (Joseph Joubert).

Often our understanding of justice includes the concept of being "fair"— and what is fair? To borrow from an ancient adage, perhaps it might be said that fair is meeting goodness with goodness, evil with justice, and all things and all people with love.

In *You and the Law* it is recalled: "The Honourable James C. McRuer, former Chief Justice of Ontario, once wrote that although justice is a term that could be no more precisely defined than love or hate or charity, it is clearly something that the human heart acknowledges."

The concluding paragraph of Mr. Justice Zuber's report to the Attorney General on the Ontario court system is a fitting end to this introduction:

> If some of the recommendations in this report do not find favour with the governing authorities, then other recommendations should be devised and implemented promptly. It would be wrong to confuse action with an endless circle of further studies, analyses, and reports which would likely do little more than lead to eventual paralyses; at this point we would do well to recall an ancient teaching:
>
> "God is urgent about justice; for upon justice the world depends…"

1 ORIGINS OF ADR

*Inventor's motto: If you don't see
what you want, make it.*
—Anonymous

EXTENSIVE SOCIOLOGICAL LITERATURE and other non-juridical accounts offer many insights on the origins of ADR. For example, an article in 1971 describing how an African tribe dealt with its disputes led to the formation of neighbourhood justice centres in the U.S. However, this chapter's succinct description will focus only on the origins of ADR as it pertains to the legal and contemporary order. The texts cited include three from U.S. sources—an academic, a lawyer and a judge—and one from a Canadian source.

The origin of the term Alternative Dispute Resolution and its acronym ADR has been attributed to the 1976 Pound Conference.[1] At that conference Warren E. Burger, Chief Justice of the U.S. Supreme Court from 1969 to 1986, delivered the keynote address, "Agenda for 2000 A.D.," calling for the creation of informal dispute resolution processes.

Chief Justice Burger is generally considered to be the founder of the ADR movement and alternatives to litigation.[2] Throughout his term in office he was an advocate for court reform, repeatedly calling on the bar to find alternatives to court adjudication.

But what must be noted is that Chief Justice Burger invited another pioneer of the ADR movement, Professor Frank E.A. Sander of Harvard University, to deliver the threshold paper "Varieties of Dispute Processing" at the 1976 Pound Conference.[3] Sander's paper marked a defining moment in the development of the ADR movement. It is only fitting to open this chapter with the following history of ADR written by Professor Sander:

---

1 See Jerome T. Barrett with Joseph P. Barrett, *A History of Dispute Resolution: The Story of a Political, Cultural and Social Movement,* p. 182.

2 I met Chief Justice Burger in 1991 and he later confirmed this history in a letter from his office.

3 In April 2010 Professor Sander confirmed this history with me.

UNITED STATES

AN ACADEMIC'S ACCOUNT

Professor Sander's brief history of ADR appeared in the *University of Florida Law Review* in 1985 while he was a member of the American Bar Association (ABA) ADR Committee. Professor Sander is also the originator of the multi-door court program:

> Beginning in the late sixties, American society witnessed an extraordinary flowering of interest in alternative forms of dispute settlement. This interest emanated from a wide variety of sources, ranging from the Chief Justice of the United States Supreme Court to corporate general counsel, the organized Bar and various lay groups. Following a decade or so of virtually unabashed enthusiasm, serious questions and doubts are now being raised. Additionally, we are slowly accumulating limited data concerning viable models and empirical effects. Hence, this may be an opportune time for evaluating and exploring promising future directions.
>
> Perhaps a good place to begin is with some definitions. What exactly do we mean by "alternative dispute resolution mechanisms" (ADRMs)? Alternative to what? Presumably "alternative" is used as a substitute for the traditional dispute resolution mechanism, the court. Interestingly enough, however, courts do not resolve most disputes. The literature on dispute processing and dispute transformation has delineated ways in which grievances may be turned into ongoing disputes, and the myriad ways in which disputes may be resolved by means other than court adjudication. In fact, disputes that cannot be readily adjudicated may be presented initially to a whole host of dispute processors such as arbitrators, mediators, fact-finders or ombudsmen. If the dispute is ultimately filed in court, approximately 90–95 percent of these disputes are settled by negotiation, with little or no court litigation. Hence, the argument for "alternatives" is not based on the need to find a substitute for court adjudication. Rather, it is based on the need to gain a better understanding of the functioning of these alternative mechanisms and processes.
>
> Alternatives to courts are not a new phenomenon. Yet, the current resurgence of alternative dispute resolution seems to have a freshness about it. The movement appears to have a much broader theoretical and practical base. It might therefore be useful briefly to speculate on the confluence of events that have led to the current renewal of interest in alternatives.
>
> The sixties were characterized by considerable strife and conflict, emanating in part from the civil rights struggles and Vietnam War protests. An apparent legacy of those times was a lessened tolerance and a greater tendency to turn grievances into disputes. Also relevant was a significant increase in the statutory creation of new causes of action.
>
> A noteworthy development from these events was that courts found themselves inundated with new filings, triggering cries of alarm from the judicial admin-

istration establishment. This judicial congestion led to claims that equal access to justice had been denied. Spurred in part by these conditions, parties [sought various alternative legal] mechanisms. In the 1964 *Civil Rights Act*, Congress established the Community Relations Service in the United States Department of Justice to aid courts and others in settling intractable racial and community disputes. The Ford Foundation established the National Center for Dispute Settlement and the Institute of Mediation and Conflict Resolution to study dispute settlement mechanisms.

Any attempt to isolate the roots of a complex and ill-understood movement is bound to suffer from oversimplification. One can readily identify a number of other social forces that contributed to the recent flowering of the alternatives movement. One contributor is the waning role of some of society's traditional mediating institutions such as the family, the church, and the ward heeler. A second influence is the discernible recent mood of anti-professionalism. Both these conditions point towards the creation of alternative indigenous mechanisms such as community mediation centers and family settlement tribunals. Of course, need alone does not always lead to constructive solutions. Fortunately for the alternatives movement the Law Enforcement Assistance Administration (LEAA) took a firm interest in developing and testing ADRMs, even if the required nexus with the criminal law system at times distorted the proper emphasis.

Certain intellectual developments paralleled these social forces. Over the past 15–20 years some cultural anthropologists have attempted to apply their study of foreign dispute settlement to the local scene. Contemporaneous with that effort has been the work of other legal scholars, most notably the late Lon Fuller, who have attempted to analyze characteristics of various dispute processes such as mediation and arbitration. These scholars proposed some useful conclusions about the strengths and limitations of particular processes for particular types of disputes.

From this brief and fragmentary history, four goals of the alternatives movement emerge:

1. to relieve court congestion, as well as undue cost and delay;
2. to enhance community involvement in the dispute resolution process;
3. to facilitate access to justice;
4. to provide more "effective" dispute resolution.

These goals might overlap and conflict. Consider, for example, the problem of "excessive" access. If society is too ready to provide access for all kinds of disputes, this will lengthen the queue and aggravate the congestion problem. Similarly, measures aimed at relieving court congestion would take a very different form from measures designed to enhance community control over dispute settlement. Hence, it is essential to think clearly and precisely about the reasons for pursuing ADRMs.

Considering the complex social conditions that have led to court congestion and concomitant delay, it seems specious to assume an appropriate use of alternatives can significantly affect court case loads. This is not to say that a cautious and informed used of ancillary mechanisms to screen court cases is not worth undertaking. On the contrary, such a program holds considerable promise. But the notion that a pervasive use of arbitration and mediation will solve "the court crisis" seems misguided. The principal promise of alternatives stems from the third and fourth goals set forth above. Our primary efforts should be directed toward these two goals. And since the access goal can only be fulfilled by providing access to an ADRM that is appropriate for the particular dispute, the third and fourth goals in effect coalesce.

Current Types of Disputes and Programs

This section presents a brief overview of the rich variety of ADRMs presently in use. Of necessity the picture will be somewhat fragmentary and conclusory. Because many mechanisms involve a blend or sequence of different dispute processes, it might be useful first to provide a brief restatement of the basic processes.

The most common and familiar form of dispute settlement between two parties is bargaining or negotiation. Negotiation offers the great advantage of allowing the parties themselves to control the process and the solution. Sometimes, however, disputants are unable to settle the dispute, and a third party must be engaged. If a third party joins the negotiations, the parties must determine whether he or she has power to impose a solution on the parties, or whether the third party is simply to help the disputants arrive at their own solution. The latter role is commonly referred to as conciliation or mediation. The former might entail some form of adjudication, by a court, an administrative agency, or a private adjudicator, also known as an arbitrator.

A LAWYER'S ACCOUNT

The following excerpt provides a different angle on the origins of ADR in the U.S.A. The excerpt is from a journal paper presented to the Association Internationale des Jeunes Avocats (known in English as the International Young Lawyers Association) in Munich, Germany on September 7, 1988 (see Chapter 6 for a more detailed report on this conference), and prepared by Gabe Shawn Varges of the New York State Bar:

> This ADR thing, it's a fad, I tell you. There is nothing it can get you that you can't get with a good lawsuit. And there is a lot you can lose—like a big settlement or a generous judgment for your client. Hell, what client will keep you if at the first sign of a dispute you start talking negotiation and mediation? Hardball, hard law, that's what your clients want and what will keep us employed.

Introduction

Until recently in the United States, it was common for proponents of alternative dispute resolution (ADR) to encounter entrenched opposition, such as that colorfully expressed (above) by a major New York litigator. The belief commonly shared among opponents was that the ADR movement either sought to replace lawyers or to force them to behave in ways contrary to how lawyers are supposed or required to behave. Although the protection of client interests was often proffered as the grounds for opposition, it was clear that many so-called "alternatives" [were met] with a certain degree of self-interested suspicion.

Today there is growing evidence that the ideas behind the ADR movement are beginning to gain acceptance in the U.S. even at the highest echelons of the legal profession. This is true even though in some parts of the country and in certain functional areas the ADR movement has yet to make its formal entrance. Nonetheless, there are indications that experimentation with ADR methods is at an all-time high in America and that the prospects for future growth in the area are good. As one noted negotiation scholar has observed, in the U.S. "conflict is a growth industry."

This paper summarizes the process by which the ADR movement has gained momentum in the U.S. and describes briefly the various dispute-settlement procedures it has given rise to. It concludes by discussing the opportunities for involvement therein for lawyers and by presenting a list of major outstanding issues and questions relating to the ADR movement today.

For the non-American lawyer a look at the American ADR scene may be useful for at least two reasons. First, it permits comparison with what has occurred and is being tried in his or her country. And second, it may be of assistance in the event he or she comes to face a dispute which is subject to any one of the many alternative dispute settlement procedures being used in the U.S. By being at least conversant with the field, the non-American lawyer will be able to better advise his or her client and work more effectively with American local counsel.

It merits mentioning that the ADR movement should not be of interest only to litigators. Indeed, the subject should be of equivalent interest to general practitioners and to family, corporate, finance, anti-trust and securities lawyers, among others. Not only has the ADR movement penetrated all these areas but increasingly the non-litigator is being asked to draft contractual clauses to provide for non-traditional dispute settlement and to advise when disputes arise thereunder.

> New Client: "So as you can see this company has cheated me. I want you to sue it and get me justice."
>
> Lawyer: "Yes, Mr. Ames. But tell me, just how much justice can you afford?"

I. Development of the American ADR Movement

A. THE ROOTS

In its most recent history, the ADR movement in the United States may be said to be an extension of the legal reform movement of the 1960s. This movement sought to improve a legal system that was commonly perceived as having become accessible only to the very wealthy. The reforms for making "justice" more affordable for the poor and working classes included introducing legal aid schemes, facilitating class actions, and creating certain specialized courts and agencies to deal with the problems of ordinary citizens (small claim courts, consumer protection agencies, legal hotlines, etc.).

Although successful in many respects, the above approaches encountered many limitations as to reach, effectiveness, and cost. These limitations, along with a growing concern with the apparent "litigation explosion" taking place in America, led many legal reformers to rethink their strategies. What gain was there to increase access to the courts if the courts already could not cope with the number of disputes being brought? What point in bringing a dispute to court if the judgment rendered further alienated the parties? And what good was attained by making use of an expensive legal system whose costs were already straining private and public resources? The answer, it seemed, was in finding solutions that brought not more but less cases to the courts, that involved not more but less law, and that generally simplified the legal process.

B. EMERGENCE OF THE MODERN MOVEMENT

Thus the American ADR movement in its modern form emerged in the early 1970s. Without abandoning the concerns of the 1960s, the ADR movement raised new questions and issues about the legal system, such as the suitability of traditional litigation for certain types of disputes, the micro and macro costs of the legal process, and the role of law and lawyers in general in society.

These broad concerns reflected the diverse composition of the movement. It included practitioners and scholars of various backgrounds, such as social workers, psychologists, anthropologists and even economists. Although lawyers were involved and played a major role in the movement, the lawyers initially active tended to be academics, those involved in providing community services to the poor, and those disenchanted with the legal system.

C. ADR GOALS

The ADR reformers had three principal goals: (1) to offer those not wishing to use the regular courts the option of alternative institutions and procedures of dispute settlement; (2) to educate the public about such alternatives; and (3) to reform the regular litigation process to make it more efficient, less costly, and more responsive to the needs of litigants. In other words, the ADR proponents hoped to divert cases out of court whenever possible and to improve the handling of those cases which did make it to court.

Following extensive efforts to raise awareness about the need for alternatives, ADR proponents succeeded in persuading courts and legislatures in various parts of the country to experiment with the proposals in a number of different areas. Dispute settlement alternatives emerged in the consumer, family, business, medical, and even environmental areas. Those working with alternatives argued that in comparison to traditional litigation the alternatives tended to be quicker, less expensive, less damaging to the relationship of the disputants, and more likely to yield creative, imaginative solutions to difficult problems. Many parties, particularly business disputants, also liked the privacy the alternatives offered.

The experiments attracted considerable attention. By the late 1970s some law schools began teaching about the alternatives (followed later by actual practical training in the area) and by 1980 the U.S. Congress voted to fund pilot projects and research on the subject.

D. Involvement by Lawyers

With the above developments, more and more mainstream lawyers become exposed to the ADR movement. Initial fears that the ADR movement sought to replace lawyers or to dismantle the adversarial system diminished as lawyers saw opportunities for involvement and recognized that the alternatives complemented rather than displaced traditional litigation. Further, public-minded lawyers came to realize that by encouraging parties to settle disputes with minimal court involvement, judicial resources were freed for those cases which truly required court adjudication.

Although hesitant at first, bar association and professional lawyer groups gradually began giving substantive attention to the phenomenon. Various working groups on the subject were created under bar sponsorship in the late 1970s and early 1980s. The American Bar Association appointed in 1982 a special committee on dispute resolution which, three years later, was turned into a standing committee whose purpose was to "study, experiment with, disseminate information concerning, and support the appropriate institutionalization of (alternative) methods for the resolution of disputes." In the meantime, a number of journals specialized on the subject of alternatives had begun appearing, and various private groups had begun offering services for those seeking an alternative to the state courts.

E. Summary

Although its origins may go back far in U.S. history, the modern American ADR movement emerged in the 1970s following the legal reform movement of the 1960s. Since that time the ADR movement has gone through two principal stages: (1) "consciousness raising" about the need to try new methods for settling disputes; and (2) implementation and experimentation with some of these new methods. The proponents of and participants in these methods have also expanded to include not only academics and community reformers, but judges, legislators, corporate executives and Wall Street lawyers.

II. ADR Procedures and Mechanisms

A. Conceptual Framework

All societies have mechanisms for resolving disputes and for coping with conflict. What form these mechanisms take, who is involved in them (who can use them and who runs them), what matters they handle, and how effective they are in reaching their goals, is reflective of the normative values of the society and the importance it attaches to certain disputes.

In the U.S. the efforts of the ADR proponents and participants have expanded considerably the options available to disputants in many parts of the country. Whereas previously the only choice many disputants effectively had was either to ignore the dispute or bring a lawsuit (often a prohibitively expensive proposition), today there are more in-between alternatives which are beginning to affect the way laypeople and lawyers think of conflict resolution.

The alternatives are making it possible to view dispute resolution more and more as a continuum on which a number of options, from the least formal to the most formal, are available for use. On the continuum, litigation is not one of the first but one of the last options. The chart appearing [in Appendix A] (the *Dispute Resolution Continuum*) illustrates this concept graphically. This chart will be referred to throughout the rest of this paper.

B. THREE TRACKS

The range of alternative mechanisms and procedures being tried in the U.S. allows for a further conceptual refinement. On the Dispute Resolution Continuum, three distinct tracks (the horizontal lines) can be identified: a non-judicial, a quasi-judicial, and a judicial track.

[Beginning] with the starting point of a dispute on the left hand side and moving toward the right, it can be seen that parties have a choice not only as to which track to take to find a solution but which mechanism to use along the way. As one moves from left to right, the mechanisms generally become more formal and structured. In between mechanisms on different tracks, one can see the relative formalism of each by its place in the numerical order. Thus the least formal mechanism is number 1, the next is number 2, etc.

To be noted is that movement between the tracks is possible. In other words, the use of one option on one track does not necessarily preclude the use of another option on another track. For example, a party who selects non-binding mediation on the non-judicial track (number 6) may still file suit through the judicial track if the mediation does not work or yield a satisfactory result. Some options, however, do preclude recourse to other options. Arbitration (number 11), for instance, typically cannot be abandoned for another option once started unless a legal challenge to the process itself is brought or unless the disputants agree together to terminate the arbitration.

To be noted as well is that three distinct modes of dispute settlement exist, regardless of which track one is on. These are marked by the vertical dotted lines.

One mode involves the disputants attempting to settle the dispute on their own (including at their option their counsel). Mechanisms for this exist on both the non-judicial and quasi-judicial tracks.

A second mode involves the disputants making use of a third party to assist them in resolving the dispute. This third party could be, for example, a private expert (on the non-judicial track), a court-appointed mediator (on the quasi-judicial track), or even a judge in a pre-trial conference (on the judicial track). The nature of that assistance and its consequences (whether binding or not on the parties) depend on the specific mechanism used.

The third mode involves the disputants seeking a legal judgment on a dispute, i.e., court adjudication. This mode, naturally found only on the judicial track, is the most structured, legally formal, and public of the choices available.

C. The Non-Judicial Track

Parties with a dispute may start anywhere in their search for a solution. Most parties, though not all, will attempt to negotiate first before taking further steps. When they do, they step on the non-judicial track.

A Judge's Account

The following account of the background to ADR in the United States was written by Judge Frank G. Evans, Chief Justice, First Judicial District Court of Appeals in Houston, Texas. This excerpt is from a paper presented at the ABA annual conference in Toronto on August 10, 1988:

ADR and the American Justice System

When we read articles about alternative dispute resolution, we may conclude that the concept is of relatively recent origin. Actually, the concept has been around for a long while; only its widespread recognition has been slow in coming.

Current recognition of the benefits of alternative dispute resolution stems from the 1976 Pound Conference, which focused on court costs and delay. At that conference, judges, lawyers and professors from across the nation met to consider the "access to justice" problems caused by the so-called "litigation explosion."

Dispute Resolution Centers

On the heels of the Pound Conference, the U.S. Department of Justice, led by then U.S. Attorney General Griffin Bell, funded three experimental "neighborhood justice centers" in Atlanta, Kansas City and Los Angeles. These dispute centers provided mediation and related services to citizens with "minor disputes." During this same time period, the Night Prosecutor's Program, a city-operated dispute resolution centre, was initiated in Columbus, Ohio, and the ABA established a new "Special Committee on Alternative Dispute Resolution of Minor Disputes." In the years that followed, "local" dispute resolution systems sprang up throughout the United States, each with its own unique personality, depending upon its sponsorship, funding, and procedural framework. Most of these dispute resolution systems had two related goals: (1) to provide a more expeditious and less costly means for citizens to resolve their conflicts; and (2) the alleviation of overcrowded court dockets.

Initially, these alternative dispute resolution centers tended to limit their services to "traditional" forums of alternative dispute resolution. Some were based entirely on the arbitration process, while others offered only mediation services,

Also, these early centers tended to process only specific types of disputes; some focused on commercial litigation, others on landlord/tenant or consumer/merchant conflicts, while still others centered their efforts on family law or child custody disputes. As these centers expanded, so did their menu of services. Today, most dispute resolution centers provide a wide variety of ADR processes and cover the whole gamut of human conflicts.

The pioneering efforts of these early alternative dispute resolution programs foretold the eventual success of the ADR movement in the United States. Their experience established beyond question that most disputes could be resolved through reasonable settlement negotiations, and at a much smaller cost to the disputants. It is not surprising that ADR users have expressed great satisfaction with the process.

Time and cost savings have not been the only reasons for user satisfaction. The ADR process offers an additional plus: the opportunity for the disputants to participate in the resolution process, to actively engage in the settlement negotiations. Because disputants can be active players in the resolution of their conflicts, they become part of the solution and are much more satisfied with the results.

As the ADR centers became more experienced, and expanded their services, another problem surfaced: how could these ADR processes be institutionalized, and how could ADR processes be incorporated as part of the formal justice system? In the 1980s ADR had only a small following, and most judges and lawyers, not to mention most laypersons, were woefully unaware of the ADR choices available to them.

Responding to this problem, Harvard law professor Frank E.A. Sander envisioned a multi-door courthouse, in which a person could obtain an assessment of his or her particular dispute and a referral to the appropriate process, or "door," to settle the dispute. In 1985 the American Bar Association Standing Committee on Alternative Dispute Resolution transformed this multi-door concept into an experimental program, and provided the incentive for multi-door programs in Washington, D.C., Tulsa, Oklahoma, and Houston, Texas.

CANADA

The Canadian experience with ADR is detailed in an excerpt of an article written by Russell L. Horrocks, which appeared in the *Alberta Law Review* in 1982. Horrocks was executive director of the Windsor-Essex Mediation Centre, a three-year joint project of the Canadian Bar Association (CBA) and the Donner Foundation that began while Gordon Henderson was president of the CBA. The work of the Windsor-Essex centre offers an example of collaborative work between lawyers and non-lawyers in this field. The grant application to the Donner Foundation, as I understand the background, was reviewed by Dean Peachey, a mediator with the Network for Community Justice and Conflict Resolution.

The Windsor-Essex project remains the most important ADR experiment and model in Canada, and indeed the Dispute Resolution Centre for Ottawa-Carleton extensively used it as a model for its methodology and objectives. Unfortunately no government funding was available to the Windsor-Essex initiative after the three-year project was completed and evaluated, and it ceased operation in 1984.[4] Interestingly, John Jennings, Q.C., who was directly involved in the Windsor-Essex project through the CBA, is slated to be the next president of the CBA. He was also very helpful to us when we started up our local initiatives in Ottawa-Carleton. Gordon Henderson is acting as chairman of the board of governors of the Canadian Institute for Conflict Resolution, the national charitable institute that grew out of these local initiatives.

In some ways the initiatives in Ottawa-Carleton are our own example (by accident of destiny, not design) of a phoenix bird that has arisen from the ashes of the Windsor-Essex project. Perhaps the adage is true that whatever goes around comes around. One source of reassurance during these times of change is that it's not the duration of the messenger but the durability of the message that provides the underlying foundation.

In Ontario the Attorney General himself has openly questioned the "underpinnings" of our legal system in order to take steps to strengthen it. As quoted in the July 1987 edition of *The Lawyers Weekly*, the Attorney General said the system is "very near the verge of collapse…(failing)…to meet the expectations of the public or (to) do justice for the vast majority of citizens."

In response to this current state of affairs, let us now consider the following account by Russell Horrocks on the development of ADR in Canada:

> It is interesting to note that alternatives to formal court procedures have always existed in society. In traditional societies an elder within a family was frequently called upon to fulfill various functions of mediation, conciliation and even arbitration in certain circumstances. Depending on the nature of the dispute, it was not uncommon to have formal procedures conducted by village elders.
>
> Professor Harry Arthurs, in an address to the Conference on the Cost of Justice (Canadian Institute for the Administration of Justice, 15 November 1979), related some historical experience with respect to the machinery of justice. In particular, Professor Arthurs traced the history of the court of requests and described the situation in 1787 where citizens sat as lay commissioners receiving no compensation for their services on the bench. Together with volunteer judges in cities, towns and

---

4 Because of budget cuts DRCOC closed its doors in 1999 after handling approximately 2,000 files for minor criminal offences. Although it's encouraging that DRCOC's tenure was three times as long as that of the Windsor-Essex project, the budget cuts illustrate how little forethought goes into the allocation of resources in our society. Research shows that mediation processes actually help reduce the human and economic costs of conflict and that people who go through a mediation process are much less likely to be involved in a future dispute.

villages across England, the lay commissioners brought to most ordinary people the only kind of civil justice they would ever receive. These local courts were much less expensive than the formal system at Westminster and perhaps more important, were mandated to decide cases according to "equity and good conscience," with the result that they often appeared to have been influenced by a spirit of mediation, situation equity, and responsiveness to local community expectations and relationships. Arthurs concluded that: "The formal system identified legal winners and losers, but contributed nothing to maintenance of the social fabric."

Mr. Justice Estey of the Supreme Court of Canada first broached the subject of alternatives to the formal judicial system in a paper entitled "Theorem on Judicial Administration" which was also presented to the Conference on the Cost of Justice. In a fuller discussion of the topic in a chapter entitled "Who Needs Courts?" Mr. Justice Estey asked the following question:

Is it possible to establish a new and less formal conduit through which we can pass the smaller and simpler differences (and by far the most numerous category of disputes) and thereby channel them away from the expensive and overburdened routes?

The kind of dispute that was contemplated included such matters as petty property disputes, by-law infractions of significance to the immediate neighbourhood only, minor traffic offences, claims in simple debt for small amounts, failure to pay minor public accounts, certain aspects of automotive collision disputes and even, perhaps, the less fundamental aspects of domestic relations. Mr. Justice Estey answered the question by recommending an adaptation of the administrative tribunal concept through the revival of neighbourhood tribunals. These tribunals would engage local citizens in the community parties to a wide range of smaller-scale disputes which are of significance to the individuals concerned but not of sufficient importance to justify the engagement of the community justice machinery.

Mr. Justice Estey identified the twin benefits of (a) increased community participation in their own judicial systems; and (b) a lowering of the tax burden and the privately borne cost of going to court, which would enure to all citizens.

The first major developments in procedures for alternative measures have occurred in the criminal justice system. The programs have most frequently been described as "diversion," which has been defined by the federal Department of Justice and the Ministry of the Solicitor General of Canada as "an alternative to the traditional process of court appearance and sentence but a component of the formal criminal justice process." Diversion programs have been established in Canada over the past decade and have in many cases been based on earlier experimentation that took place in the United States.

* * *

Diversion in Canada tends to be associated with criminal activities and there are relatively fewer programs that provide alternative solutions to civil disputes. Nevertheless, there is a growing interest in fashioning programs that will provide such alternatives and, as noted, commentators such as Mr. Justice Estey and Professor Arthurs have suggested that we are simply restoring some historical practices in terms of conflict resolution.

A further reason for heightened interest in alternative civil dispute resolution is the enormous amount of activity taking place in the United States in this field. The American Bar Association Special Committee on Resolution of Minor Disputes in 1981 identified 141 active dispute resolution programs in the United States, The original motivation for establishing alternative dispute resolution forums arose because of an increasing concern in the United States over the way in which justice was being delivered. This was particularly the case with respect to the responsiveness of institutions charged with resolving, or assisting in the resolution of disputes that arise in the course of daily life. While many of these matters could appear to be of relatively small magnitude, to the individuals concerned they are often the most important matter for the moment. Collectively, they are of enormous social consequence. Thus it was considered essential that mechanisms to effectively resolve such disputes be provided.

The American Bar Association played a leading role in organizing groups which were joined in the debate regarding the court's role in dispute resolution. The ABA (in particular through its Committee on the Resolution of Minor Disputes) co-sponsored a conference with the Judicial Conference of the United States and the Conference of Chief Justices on the subject of "Causes of Popular Dissatisfaction With the Administration of Justice" (The Pound Conference). The Chairman of that Conference was Griffin Bell and when he became Attorney General of the United States in 1977 he was instrumental in starting programs known as Neighborhood Justice Centers in Atlanta, Georgia; Kansas City, Missouri; and Los Angeles, California. These programs were developed by the Department of Justice and promoted by the American Bar Association. Briefly stated, the centres were to provide third-party mediation to resolve disputes and an alternative to traditional litigation.

A review of the 141-odd alternative dispute resolution initiatives in the United States and current research suggests that mediation projects process cases rapidly, the projects appear to be viewed favourably by the disputants, the projects may be more effective than courts in resolving disputes, and the projects improve access to justice.

In Canada, the development of alternative programs has had a modest beginning. One program which falls into this category is a community mediation service that is being operated in the Kitchener-Waterloo area by the Mennonite Central Committee (Ontario). The service was established late in 1979 as a result of several years of planning and study by a committee of community persons associated with the Mennonite Central Committee (Ontario).

Several members of the Committee had participated in the founding and ongoing administration of the Victim-Offender Reconciliation Project as well as other community-based involvements in the criminal justice system in the Waterloo region. The perception of a need for a neighbourhood dispute settlement process that would operate as an alternative to the adversary system of the courts developed out of conversations with local police officers, court officials and various members of social service agencies. In addition, the committee members studied the American experiments and were impressed with the success of settling disputes before they escalated to the point of criminal activity. The Committee was convinced that mediation as a technique for resolving a broad range of minor disputes had been well established in the American programs. It was found that police and other officials were often frustrated at the amount of time required to deal with minor cases and were also ill-equipped to deal with the root of the problem, since the complaint was usually only the culmination of a series of events arising out of a malfunctioning relationship. The mediation proceeding provides an alternative forum in which disputing parties will be brought together with a neutral third party who will attempt to mediate an acceptable restructuring of the relationship. If an agreement is reached it can be reduced to writing and signed by both parties as a legally binding contract. It is felt that the mediation process allows the interests of both parties to be respected in a way that overcomes the "win-lose" circumstances which exist in the adversary process, since both parties have a personal stake in preserving the restructured relationship they themselves have helped to design. Dispute mediation programs are currently operating in the cities of Halifax and Montreal. These programs employ a variety of program models, training approaches and organization structures while sharing the underlying philosophy of establishing an informal conflict resolution process.

Under the leadership of the Kitchener-Waterloo program, a national workshop on dispute mediation was held in April 1981 in Saskatoon, Saskatchewan. This workshop was an important step in the development of the mediation process in Canada, since programs have developed largely independent of one another.

In January 1980 the Canadian Bar Foundation commenced research into the issue of costs and delays in the administration of justice. The specific research activity was undertaken with the view to devising a program directed at minimizing unnecessary delays and costs in connection with the administration of justice. A specific project was presented to the Foundation and it was accepted in principle. With further financial assistance from the Donner Canadian Foundation, the Canadian Bar Foundation established, on November 4, 1981, on a two-year pilot basis, an alternative dispute resolution centre in Windsor, Ontario known as the Windsor-Essex Mediation Centre, to test mediation and conciliation techniques in the resolution of minor civil disputes. The objectives of the project are:

a)   To minimize the delays inherent in our court system, and

b)   To provide an alternative method of dispute resolution for appropriate types of controversies, such as:

    1. simple family disputes

2. neighbourhood problems (i.e. noise, pets, nuisance)
3. landlord/tenant
4. claims in simple debt for small amounts
5. consumer/merchant
6. employer/employee

The participants to these kinds of disputes are involved in an interdependent relationship and in such cases there is a need for a voluntary process (such as mediation) that has a capacity of re-establishing the relationship between the parties rather than simply dealing with the surface systems of the relationship as the judicial process would.

★ ★ ★

Unlike the United States where the federal Department of Justice played a leading role in the original design and introduction of Neighborhood Justice Centers, [in Canada] there has been no involvement by government in the exploration of alternative techniques. Had it not been for the financial support of institutions such as the Donner Canadian Foundation there would not even be experimental programs in Canada at this time. Indeed the lack of government response to challenges and suggestions of leading members of the legal community, including Mr. Justice Estey, is mystifying and regrettable. As is the case with criminal diversion programs, there is an urgent need for government positions being established in the field of alternative civil dispute resolution.

There continue to be developments within the judicial system to employ alternative techniques. These initiatives are being developed particularly in the provinces of Ontario and British Columbia where mediation services are being employed in the small claims courts. An informal experiment started by Gordon Killeen, Chief Judge of Middlesex County Court in London, Ontario, for the mediation settlement of small claims has prompted similar experiments in Toronto and Ottawa. Settlement rates through mediation vary between 33 and 76 percent and the volume has predictably grown with the increase in the Court's monetary jurisdiction to $1,000. In London, local lawyers have been appointed deputy judges for mediation services and it is hoped that mediation may eventually be used in all Small Claims court across Ontario. In British Columbia a Small Claims court alternative dispute resolution program is underway in the Lower Fraser Valley. The program was proposed through the Office of the Chief Judge and has received Provincial Government policy and budgetary approval.

Ms. K.M. Morrison, court examiner in B.C., in a memorandum about a dispute resolution project in her jurisdiction, suggested that in the case of the Neighborhood Justice Centers in the United States, "...there has been little discussion of why such alternatives should be developed outside the existing court system; rather the tendency has been to proliferate structures rather than to improve the current machinery." Her argument is that the conciliation and mediation options should be included within the court structure.

An excellent model for alternatives being developed inside an existing court system can be found in the Province of Quebec. The Small Claims legislation is not a separate statute but is Book Eight of the *Code of Civil Procedure*, thus making it possible to deal with Small Claims within the regular law as a whole.

* * *

The resolution of disputes between merchants and their customers over the quality of goods and services by means of arbitration has been recorded since time immemorial. Various reasons have been advanced to justify the attractiveness of arbitration, including the confidential character of the proceedings, as well as parties feeling more secure in the knowledge that an arbitrator of choice will be a specialist in the area in question, capable of providing an expeditious resolution to the dispute. In each of the provinces there is some provision for the enforcement of private arbitration with Arbitration Acts having been enacted in every province but Newfoundland, where the *Judicature Act* governs, and Quebec, where the *Code of Civil Procedure* prevails. Respective ministers of justice have indicated that there is no need for federal legislation regarding arbitration, although limited provisions do exist, for example, with respect to compulsory labour arbitration under the *Public Service Staff Relations Act.*

Nevertheless, it appears that the popularity of commercial arbitration is growing in Canada. The United States Arbitration Association has reported that in 1979 it had more arbitrations involving Canadian enterprises than in any previous year. Furthermore, the Institute of Arbitrators in Canada is becoming better known and the arbitration system of the International Chamber of Commerce in Paris is universally used.

One organization which has been very active in promoting the concept of arbitration in the domestic context is the Better Business Bureau (BBB) of Canada, which currently operates an arbitration program for the resolution of consumer-business disputes in Vancouver, Edmonton, Calgary, Winnipeg, Kitchener, Windsor and Halifax (the Montreal bureau is considering the introduction of arbitration).

The experiences that individuals have with the administration of justice will profoundly affect their attitudes towards the legal system in their country. The greater the number of avenues for participation, the greater the potential for respect and confidence in the administration of justice on the part of the citizen. Citizens who actively participate in the resolution of their disputes are making a positive contribution by redirecting a matter that is not properly the subject of judicial attention, and hopefully they will arrive at a more humane and long-lasting solution.

In Canada, we are slowly moving towards a revised approach in dispute resolution within and outside the judicial system. The present approaches are by no means complete and permanent; they are partial and temporary answers in the evolution and development of Canada's social and legal institutions.

2 CONCERNS ABOUT ADR

The law must be preserved, but justice must be done.
And they are not always the same.
—I.F. Stone, *The Trial of Socrates*

"THAT'S JUSTICE!" V. "THAT'S JUSTICE?" The differences in intonation remind us that people respond to these issues in more than one way. In the great tradition of the bar, all the jurisprudence must be presented, including cases that go the other way. Hence, by analogy, this section seeks to present the main concerns of some sceptical observers about the ADR movement. In this chapter I will try to present that side of the story and seek to address from my own understanding some of the legitimate concerns that are raised.

It seems that the most quoted opponent of ADR is Owen M. Fiss, who in 1984, while he was Alexander M. Bichel Professor of Public Law at Yale University, wrote an article appropriately entitled "Against Settlement." This provocative article drew many responses from students and practitioners of ADR, including a 1985 article by Andrew McThenia and Thomas Shaffer called "For Reconciliation." And in turn, Mr. Fiss responded to the article by McThenia and Shaffer with a second article called "Out of Eden." In his response he says that in his earlier article, "I tried to come to terms with a movement that seeks alternatives to litigation...known as ADR." A Philadelphia trial lawyer, Arthur G. Raynes, who spoke at the ABA ADR seminar in Toronto in 1988, also touches upon these three articles.

In order to focus on some of the key points being raised as people try to come to terms with ADR, I will briefly deal with these three articles and other sources that capture the essence of some of the dialogue, which reveals that on both sides of the ADR debate there is little agreement as to the so-called arguments pro and con. I suggest that if we shift our explanation of this ADR movement as offering "alternatives for people" and not "alternatives to litigation" as Mr. Fiss's premise is, then perhaps we can better come to terms with what is happening.

Mr. Fiss states that this movement which is now "sweeping the bar" was headed by Chief Justice Burger as a result of his famous 1982 proclamation, "Isn't There a Better Way?", which followed his 1976 treatise called "Agenda for 2000 A.D.—A Need for Systematic Anticipation." Chief Justice Burger, Fiss continues, received "the endorsement" of Derek Bok, President of Harvard University. Having established his premise and identified the eminent supporters of ADR, Mr. Fiss then takes them on.

Mr. Fiss argues that settlement is the "civil analogue to plea bargaining" and is a "highly problematic technique for streamlining dockets." Some of his main concerns are an imbalance of power between parties; the absence of authoritative consent, especially when the disputants are groups or organizations; lack of appropriate policing mechanisms for settlements; and "the lack of a foundation for continuing judicial involvement," on the reasoning that "the dispute-resolution story trivializes the remedial dimensions of lawsuits and mistakenly assumes judgment to be the end of the process."

The following excerpts highlight some of Mr. Fiss's other main arguments, that litigation is meant to secure justice not peace, that there is more to lawsuits than the myopia of stating that only 5 to 10% go to trial, and that a lawsuit is not simply a private matter but should be seen in public terms as having fundamental importance to society:

> To be against settlement is not to urge that parties be "forced" to litigate, since that would interfere with their autonomy and distort the adjudicative process; the parties will be inclined to make the court believe that their bargain is justice. To be against settlement is only to suggest that when parties settle, society gets less than what appears, and for a price it does not know it is paying. Parties might settle while leaving justice undone. The settlement of a school suit might secure the peace, but not racial equality. Although the parties are prepared to live under the terms they bargained for, and although such peaceful coexistence may be a necessary precondition of justice, and itself a state of affairs to be valued, it is not justice itself. To settle for something means to accept less than some ideal.

> I recognize that judges often announce settlements not with a sense of frustration or disappointment, as my account of adjudication might suggest, but with a sigh of relief. But this sigh should be seen for precisely what it is: It is not a recognition that a job is done, nor an acknowledgement that a job need not be done because justice has been secured. It is instead based on another sentiment altogether, namely that another case has been "moved along," which is true whether or not justice has been done. Or the sigh might be based on the fact that only the judgment has been avoided.

> To all this, one can readily imagine a simple response by way of confession and avoidance: We are not talking about those lawsuits. Advocates of ADR might insist that my account of adjudication, in contrast to the one implied by the dispute-resolution story, focuses on a rather narrow category of lawsuits. They could argue

that while settlement may have only the most limited appeal with respect to those cases, I have not spoken to the "typical" case.

Someone like Bok sees adjudication in essentially private terms: The purpose of lawsuits and the civil courts is to resolve disputes, and the amount of litigation we encounter is evidence of the needlessly combative and quarrelsome character of Americans. Or as Bok put it, using a more diplomatic idiom: "At bottom, ours is a society built on individualism, competition, and success." I, on the other hand, see adjudication in more public terms: Civil litigation is an institutional arrangement for using state power to bring a recalcitrant reality closer to our chosen ideals. We turn to the courts because we need to, not because of some quirk in our personalities. We train our students in the tougher arts so that they may help secure all that the law promises, not because we want them to become gladiators or because we take a special pleasure in combat.

To conceive of the civil lawsuit in public terms as America does might be unique. I am willing to assume that no other country—including Japan, Bok's new paragon—has a case like *Brown* v. *Board of Education* [landmark 1954 U.S. Supreme Court decision that struck down state laws on racial segregation in schools] in which the judicial power is used to eradicate the caste structure. I am willing to assume that no other country conceives of law and uses law in quite the way we do. But this should be a source of pride rather than shame. What is unique is not the problem, that we live short of our ideals, but that we alone among the nations of the world seem willing to do something about it. Adjudication American-style is not a reflection of our combativeness but rather a tribute to our inventiveness and perhaps even more to our commitment.

In his second article, "Out of Eden," Professor Fiss complains about the "religious dimension" that was added to the ADR discussion by professors McThenia and Shaffer, in their "For Reconciliation" article in favour of ADR. He argues as follows:

> Adjudication is more likely to do justice than conversation, mediation, arbitration, settlement, rent-a-judge, mini-trials, community moots or any other contrivance of ADR, precisely because it vests the power of the state in officials who act as trustees for the public, who are highly visible, and who are committed to reason. What we need at the moment is not another assault on this form of public power, whether from the periphery or the center, or whether inspired by religion or politics, but a renewed appreciation of all that it promises.

McThenia and Shaffer, however, warned that we should be suspect of those "who believe in law and in nothing else" and conclude that "what (we) do not need, and the community does not need is an argument that reduces the alternatives to a caricature." It seems that Fiss's complaint is to their thinking, which is exemplified in their statement: "Justice is what we discover—you and I, Socrates said—when we walk together, listen together, and even love one another, in our curiosity about what justice is and where justice comes from." They add this footnote:

Professor Milner S. Ball, who discussed this comment with us, suggested that Fiss is not arguing so much against religious or community-based ADR as against dereg- ulation. Fiss may, Ball suggests, be asking us to consider whether an overly enthu- siastic support of settlement is not another form of the deregulation movement, one that permits private actors with powerful economic interests to pursue self- interest free of community norms. We may, Ball suggests, be reacting to Fiss's over- ly inclusive statements about ADR; he may have overstated, and we may have over-reacted. Thus, we may have more common ground than we think. Ball's sug- gestion is one we will enjoy pursuing. When we do, we will want to tell Ball that the powerful economic interests are as much members of the fragmented but also reconciling community as the oppressed are. And we will want to tell Fiss that it may make a general and important difference that, in almost any kind of ADR, (a) the parties talk to one another, rather than to the government; and that (b) the third party, if there is one present, comes not as a resolver of disputes but as a neighbor."

McThenia and Shaffer's understanding of Fiss's argument is as follows:

Fiss is against settlement because he views the matters that comes before courts in America, and that are inappropriate for ADR, as including cases in which: (1) there are distributional inequities; (2) securing authoritative consent or settlement is difficult; (3) continued supervision following judgment is necessary; and (4) there is a genuine need for an authoritative interpretation of law. Fiss characterizes disputes in this limited way—as arguments between two neighbors, one of whom has vastly superior bargaining power over the other. It is then easy for him to pre- fer litigation to settlement, because litigation is a way to equalize bargaining power."

In his paper at the 1988 ABA Conference in Toronto, Arthur G. Raynes of the Philadelphia Bar saw the growing usefulness of the famous "principled negotiation" theories of Fisher and Ury in Getting to Yes, "focusing on the inter- est of the parties rather than their legal positions and therefore the practical usefulness for the lawyers of these skills."

Mr. Raynes rightly states that the "proponents of ADR need not 'trash...' courts and trial lawyers to argue persuasively that society benefits from a broader array of dispute options." He warns that the credibility of ADR pro- ponents is not heightened by their lashing out at American litigants as being afflicted with "some form of mass neurosis that leads many people to think courts were created to solve all the problems of mankind" (referring to an address by former Chief Justice Warren Burger in 1985). Citing McThenia and Shaffer's "For Reconciliation" article, Mr. Raynes also correctly notes: "Nor is the messianic tone assumed by some ADR proponents likely to endear its goals and methods to trial lawyers." He laments that "it does not warm any trial lawyer's heart to read comments like, 'repeatedly these days, prominent jurists (including members of the Supreme Court) say that litigation and lawyers are bad'" (citing a 1986 article by Judith Resnick, "Failing Faith: Adjudicatory Procedure in Decline"), and also refers to the unfortunate comment in 1984 by James Henry, President of the Center for Public Resources in New York, that "rarely does one hear a good word said for litigation." Mr. Raynes then extols the virtues and historical and social benefits of litigation and legal precedents for the benefit of many disadvantaged. He jokingly ends with, "There, I've slain the beast."

I've cited these quotations to present a flavour of the serious split that has occurred in thinking about ADR as a social phenomenon. Elsewhere, I spoke facetiously about mediation being needed between some proponents of litigation and some proponents in ADR as it is currently explained!

Perhaps as a "Johnny-come-lately" to this field and without the benefit of exploring all of the consequences, I can more easily get away with stating again that it occurs to me that if ADR is seen as *an alternative for people* and <u>not</u> *an alternative to litigation,* the proponents of litigation and the proponents of ADR processes would find more common ground and could better work together.

In relation to the impugned elevation of the ADR issue into "messianic" tones, I have a few thoughts. First, as a friend commented in discussing this issue, surely nothing useful, permanent or understandable can be accomplished without reference to some value system. The adversarial attitude in trial is, of course, win-lose, or as academics would call it, a "zero-sum game." (A zero-sum game is, strictly speaking, one where the total winnings for one party minus the total losses for the other equals zero. See Professor Carrie Menkel-Meadow: "Toward Another View of Legal Negotiations—The Structure of Problem Solving," included in the bibliography). Of course, the win-lose approach is the value system for many of our social habits, but this book is not meant to engage in such social philosophy. However, it is important to keep our global perspective in mind, remembering that lawyering is a "human profession," as an author wrote in the Law Society of Upper Canada *Gazette*.

Simplistically, the opposite of the win-lose approach is likely to be called "win-win," but Professor Menkel-Meadow would instead call it negotiation "problem solving." She says that "in focusing on problem solving for mutual gain, the lawyer will execute one of his obligations to the society that charters his profession."

Second, why some proponents of ADR are motivated to think in spiritual or other universal terms is up to them. As Dan McCurdy, President of Surgenor Motors and a strong supporter of our local initiatives, would say, "You don't have to believe what I believe, but please believe that I believe what I believe." There should be no hidden attempt to proselytize, but people should be unashamed in making clear their beliefs. However, those who support ADR for a particular reason should not claim it fits only into their belief structure. ADR is truly apolitical and non-denominational in its attractiveness, usefulness and practical value.

This is a healthy dialogue, and trying to appreciate Mr. Fiss's provocative perspectives is really quite helpful in dealing with the issues that arise with ADR. I wonder what Mr. Fiss might think about Lord Molton's 1927 speech wherein the Lord Justice commented that the movement of a truly just and civilized society is towards "obedience to the unenforceable." This phrase contains much food for thought, and its point, I believe, is deserving of our modern-day attention. It might lead to a better understanding of these more philosophical or spiritual matters, to the extent that any one of us may be interested in them.

The philosophical or spiritual aspect of the ADR discussion is treated practically, sensitively, and sensibly by David Luban of the Center for Philosophy and Public Policy at Maryland University in his working paper, "The Quality of Justice":

> But reconciliation theories need not be religiously based.
>
> It seems evident that the kind of reconciliation, or transformation of the parties, that takes place in a mini-trial, must be characterized in more restrained terms than those we have been examining. The parties do come to appreciate the other's viewpoint when ADR succeeds; they do treat the other as a person rather than as a pothole on the highway of life. In a word, they come to respect the other. It isn't love; it may be solidarity; but it is not to be denigrated.
>
> Could a mediator or arbitrator really kick off the proceedings—an attempt to resolve a business dispute, let us say, in which both disputing parties are quite angry with each other—by announcing, "the aim of these sessions is not merely to resolve your dispute. It is to do so by transforming you so that you come to regard each other as fellow members of a loving community"?
>
> Surely the answer is no. That may be the last thing that the disputants want. They may hate each other's guts. Even if the disputants were receptive to the idea of a loving community, they would rightly suggest that the proposed transformation would be a welcome but incidental byproduct of a process, the primary aim of which is merely to resolve the dispute,
>
> There is nothing at all untoward about the mediator explaining "The aim of these sessions is not merely to settle your dispute, but to do so by getting you to appreciate and respect each other's point of view." In fact, the parties probably understand already that this is how mediation works; as Millhauser remarked, parties who don't understand this, who gird their loins with full adversarial armor when they enter ADR, are simply parties for whom ADR will fail.

ADR has also been called "mutually respectful problem solving." I hope that ADR will not just spawn another group of scholars, who, it has been said, make much of their subjects in order to make much of themselves. In a serious vein, though, it is appreciated that learning is the lifeblood towards asking the right questions.

A list of relevant questions are set out below under the heading "Cautions and Concerns," excerpted from the excellent book, *Dispute Resolution*, by Goldberg, Green and Sander. This is the first book of its type intended as a teaching tool for law students. In the book the authors cover primary processes (negotiation, mediation, and adjudication, both court and arbitration); hybrid processes (mediation-arbitration; mini-trials); binding processes, including private judges; "high-low" contracts; final offer arbitration; non-binding processes (summary jury trial, neutral expert fact finding, ombudsmen, settlement special masters); and integrated processes. At the end of the book is a section called "overcoming impediments to the use of alternative dispute resolution processes." Selected applications include family, neighbourhood justice centers, intra-institutional relationships (concentrating on employer-employee and union-management), consumers, environmental, intergovernmental, and international.

It is good that this type of text is available, evidencing the growing interest in teaching this subject in law schools. At an ever-increasing rate, other disciplines and industries, especially business schools, are incorporating conflict and dispute resolution into their curriculums and ongoing educational programs. I hope there will soon be a day when such topics are regularly available, not only in law schools and law departments of universities, but also in bar admission courses and continuing legal education sections of bar associations and law societies. It is suggested that *Without Prejudice*, the proposed educational program discussed in Chapter 5, could be a valuable coordinating vehicle for the legal profession.

Cautions and Concerns

As has already been noted, the euphoria that marked the early days of the alternatives movement has given way, at least in part, to a period of reflection. Serious questions are being raised about the implications of the movement and its future. The most important questions, which you should try to keep in mind as you go through the materials, are these:

- If the alternatives to adjudication have all the advantages claimed for them, why are they not more widely used? Are there aspects of the legal system that deter the use of alternatives? Or does the lack of demand for alternatives demonstrate that the alternatives movement is primarily a result of self-interest on the part of alternatives providers rather than an expression of the need for alternatives?

- Is there an adequate empirical basis for the claimed advantages of the alternatives? How, for example, can one adequately measure the asserted advantages of mediation over adjudication? Is it possible to develop a sophisticated cost-benefit analysis of alternative processes?

- If the alternatives possess the advantages claimed for them, then should they be made compulsory at least as a prerequisite to resort to the courts? Or would the advantages of the alternatives evaporate with their compulsory use?

- Can we develop a satisfactory taxonomy of dispute resolution processes, matching disputes to appropriate dispute resolution processes?

- Is there a danger that in our preoccupation with finding the "appropriate" dispute resolution process we will lose sight of the need for fair outcomes?

- Is there a risk that the availability of alternatives will cause a shunting of low- and middle-income disputants to a form of second-class justice consisting primarily of semi-coerced compromise settlements, while what is perceived as first-class justice, that offered by the courts, is reserved for the rich and powerful? (In thinking about this question the student should be aware that the neighborhood justice center clientele consists primarily of low-income disputants referred to the centers by courts and prosecutors for an alternative to criminal proceedings, and that court-annexed arbitration is typically required only for cases in which the amount in controversy is below $10,000 to $15,000.)

- Is there a danger that mediation, with its emphasis on accommodation and compromise, will deter large-scale structural changes in political and societal institutions that only court adjudication can accomplish, and that it will thus serve the interests of the powerful against the disadvantaged?

- To the extent that new modes of dispute resolution call for new practitioners with skills different from those who practice in the judicial system, what steps should be taken to ensure that those practitioners have the requisite skills? Should there be regulation of the practice of dispute resolution similar to that of the practice of law?

- Can the alternatives movement survive success? If alternative dispute resolution processes become widely used, will they suffer from the woes common to other heavily used institutions—increasing costs and delays, bureaucratization, and perfunctory performance?

- In light of the prominent place of the courts in American society and the free dispute resolution services provided by the courts, how can other forms of dispute resolution, even if more appropriate for a particular dispute, succeed in attracting users and adequate funding? Does the answer lie in integrating alternative dispute resolution processes into the public justice system? If so, how should this be done?

Dispute Resolution was the subject of a very insightful critical review by Sally Merry, professor of anthropology at Wellesley College, who calls its publication an important event bearing out the "growing prominence of the ADR movement." Her review raises some substantial concerns about the ADR movement;

she warns of the danger of not understanding "alternative" in the context of society and broad culture, and also warns about being naïve about the political implications while forgetting about the important matters of law in our culture. She also states that some proponents of ADR, in their enthusiasm over the discovery that law is only one alternative, fail to see stages in processes rather than alternatives, and lack a historical perspective which could, she says, essentially "red-flag" how "alternatives" can become as difficult and complex as the institutions they are meant to improve upon. (It seems that she seized the opportunity to express many vital questions to consider about ADR, but in fairness, *Dispute Resolution* was surely not meant to deal with these general issues and hence is not so much a target for her questions as a trigger.)

Professor Merry's cautionary comments have been echoed by many others, including Charles E. Ellison (at the School of Planning and Center for the Study of Dispute Resolution at the University of Cincinnati) whose opening paragraph in a conference paper nicely sets out some of the general principles behind the concerns:

> This paper is a deliberately speculative attempt to synthesize the literature critical of dispute resolution and its applications in the legal system and public policy processes. My central claim is that dispute resolution is a form of political theory and public policy that (1) inadequately analyzes the problems of democracy; (2) proposes mechanisms that are generally not consistent with democratic principles; and (3) may, therefore contribute to, rather than lessen, the legitimation problems of American democracy. In pursuing this theme, we review the state of dispute resolution programs in state and local government, ADR's diagnosis of the problems of democratic governance, dispute resolution as a form of pluralist political theory, the bureaucratic nature of dispute resolution, the ambiguities of mediation culture, the political uses of dispute resolution, and my sketch for more democratic approaches to public policy conflicts.

Another very important body of literature pertinent to the ADR issues raised by Mr. Ellison's paper is known as the Critical Legal Studies (CLS) movement, which studies how ADR might fit with the legal system. One of the leading books on the CLS movement was edited by Allan Hutchinson of Osgoode Law School at York University in Toronto. In his introduction, Mr. Hutchinson writes:

> Over the past decade, the vigorous challenge of CLS to jurisprudential orthodoxy has gained momentum and force. CLS has mounted a major offensive on the whole edifice of modern jurisprudence. CLS has waged an increasing campaign against the privileged citadel of traditional lawyering.

Another book, *Critical Legal Studies*, edited by Peter Fitzpatrick and Alan Hunt, offers this "formative statement" concerning the Conference on Critical

Legal Studies, held in the late 1970s, which is considered the origin of CLS:

> The central focus of the critical legal approach is to explore the manner in which legal doctrine and legal education and the practices of legal institutions work to buttress and support a pervasive system of oppressive, neglatarian relations. Critical theory works to develop radical alternatives, and to explore and debate the role of law in the creation of social, economic and political relations that will advance human emancipation.

But it is hoped that what will emerge from these various discussions is that the key gain of ADR is a change of attitude. The following excerpt represents just one method to help accomplish this goal. It is reprinted from the brochure called *Fighting Fair: A Guide,* published by the Conflict Resolution Network of Australia. By asking twelve simple questions, this brochure encourages better listening skills and promotes thinking in non-adversarial ways. (This brochure is an example of the literature that would be distributed to members of the educational program, *Without Prejudice,* which is discussed in Chapter 5.)

DO I WANT TO RESOLVE THE CONFLICT?
Be willing to fix the problem

CAN I SEE THE WHOLE PICTURE AND NOT JUST MY OWN POINT OF VIEW?
Broaden your outlook

WHAT ARE THE NEEDS AND ANXIETIES OF EVERYONE INVOLVED?
Write them down.

HOW CAN WE MAKE THIS FAIR?
Negotiate.

WHAT ARE THE POSSIBILITIES?
Think up as many solutions as you can.
Pick the one that gives everyone more of what they want.

CAN WE WORK IT OUT TOGETHER?
Treat each other as equals.

WHAT AM I FEELING?
Am I too emotional?
Could I get more facts, take time out to calm down, tell them how I feel?

WHAT DO I WANT TO CHANGE?
Be clear. Attack the problem, not the person.

WHAT OPPORTUNITY CAN THIS BRING?
Work on the positives, not the negatives.

WHAT IS IT LIKE TO BE IN THEIR SHOES?
Do they know I understand them?

Do we need a neutral third person?

Could this help us to understand each other and create our own solutions?

How can we both win?

Work towards solutions where everyone's needs are respected.

> (From *Fighting Fair: A Guide*. Printed by the
> Conflict Resolution Network of Australia.)

As one person in the audience at a conference warned, let's not create another set of credentials and professionals that make people doubt whether they are able to resolve their own differences, since the very opposite is the thrust of ADR. And as my teacher-friend said, in democratic theory is it not the ordinary person, the citizens, and especially our young people who are the key to understanding the point and promise of these things?

As one school of thought contends, is justice and the law a part of our political culture, if not an extension of it? In democratic thinking, isn't the objective to allow people to participate fully and freely and be able to make their own choices? Doesn't ADR in its own way seek to accomplish these ends—providing people with choices and alternatives so that democracy in theory becomes democracy in fact? And shouldn't we be searching for common ways to explain these things since the common law, claimed by some to be aristocratic in origin, emerged for the benefit of the common man? Doesn't all of the reasoning simply amount to a welcome return to common sense?[1]

With this is in mind, the many legitimate concerns about ADR may perhaps be put in better perspective: seeing ADR not so much as the growth of another institution but as the growth of individuals, both in the general public and the professions, wherein rights, control, power and dollars make way (not necessarily give way) in our dispute resolution and conflict response attitudes for interests, care, participation and dignity. Keeping in mind the admonishments of Sally Merry and others, we should try to appreciate these things in the context of or as challenges to our personal, social and cultural values.

---

1 One United States Supreme Court Justice noted that he believed judgements were only 10% rationalization to accommodate the other 90% instinct that underlies the decision. Can't we follow the lead of the "plain language" movement in legislative and contract circles and apply layman's terms to ADR? So we come full circle.

FOR FURTHER READING:

Kohn, Alfie. "It's Hard to Get Left Out of a Pair," *Psychology Today,* October 1987.

National Institute for Dispute Resolution. "Getting to Yes—Six Years Later, " Interviews with Roger Fisher and William Ury. NIDR news publication, May 1987.

Pruitt, Dean G. "Solutions Not Winners," *Psychology Today,* December 1987.

Rabow, Gerald. "The Co-operative Edge," *Psychology Today,* January 1988.

Schlossberg, Nancy K. "Taking the Mystery out of Change," *Psychology Today,* May 1987.

Socks, Howard R. "Alternative Dispute Resolution Movement: Wave of the Future or Flash in the Pan?" *Alberta Law Review* XXVI, no. 2.

3 ADR—ALTERNATIVE TO WHAT OR FOR WHOM?

One man's justice is another's injustice.
–Ralph Waldo Emerson, *Essays*

ONE INTERESTING ASPECT of this alternative dispute resolution movement is the struggle to explain the name. For historical and good reasons, it seems that "alternative" has come to be accepted as meaning *alternatives to litigation*. Also, it seems that despite attempts to create another label for this movement (e.g., BDR–Better Dispute Resolution), the term ADR is embedded in the professional terminology and is here to stay. This was also the opinion of Dr. Glossner, Chair of the ADR Committee of the International Bar Association at the Association Internationale des Jeunes Avocats (AIJA) in Munich, Germany. The following quotations from two recent working papers confirm this perspective:

> ...ADR procedures should be measured against the anticipated result of a trial–the so-called "shadow-verdict." After all, the reasoning goes, ADR is *alternative* dispute resolution, and adjudication is what ADR is alternative to. [1]

> In the most recent period, the ADR movement has been given a special boost by the "discovery" of and responses to, the "litigation explosion."[2]

It may be appropriate here to once again note the view of some litigation practitioners on the meaning of the ADR name. At one workshop, Mr. Frederick L. Myers of Osler Hoskin & Harcourt in Toronto neatly referred to litigation as "forced negotiation." Mr. William McMurtry at Toronto's Blaney McMurtry Stapells included the following about ADR in a May 1988 address to the Canadian Bar Association:

---

1 David Luban, "The Quality of Justice."

2 Susan Selby and Austin Sarat, "Dispute Processing in Law and Legal Scholarship: From Institutional Critique to the Reconstitution of the Judicial Subject."

In litigation particularly, look for not only reasonable early settlements but, wherever possible, innovative or alternative ways of resolving disputes. A.D.R. is the new "buzz-word" of the profession with all its sophisticated alternatives. For many practitioners there is really nothing new to the concept. It is nothing more than a realization that the traditional adversary system with its exorbitant costs, unrealizable delays and often bizarre and unpredictable results, is not the best means of resolving most disputes between intelligent and responsible parties. In my experience there are many excellent litigation counsel who have practised over the past two decades with this assumption in mind. If someone is being dishonest or totally unreasonable or there is a new area of law to be determined, then the courtroom is available and it can be a useful and exciting experience. However, for the vast majority of cases, to end up in the courtroom is an indication of failure of the system. It is often blamed on one or both of the parties but, in my experience, in most cases the blame resides with one or more of the counsel involved.

For some reason, there are many in our profession who believe that showing too much reasonableness or objectivity at the outset of a lawsuit is a sign of weakness that somehow will be used against you later if the matter cannot be settled. Again, this has not been my experience. I am most comfortable and content to end up in the courtroom confident with the knowledge that from the outset of the litigation we have maintained a reasonable and objective position and have not postured unrealistically in the hopes of attracting a favourable settlement.

It is always a matter of interest to me that you can almost predict the course of a particular lawsuit, depending not so much on who the parties are, but rather the counsel representing them. From personal knowledge I know that some of the best courtroom lawyers in this province are also among the most reasonable and objective when it comes to evaluating their cases. Almost without exception, any time you are involved with these particular individuals, you can anticipate an early, reasonable and amicable settlement. Unfortunately these individuals are in the minority.

The basic problem with the adversary system is that it tends to unnecessarily polarize the parties. Many litigation counsel view themselves as "hired guns" looking for the dramatic shootout where the opposition is vanquished. Hopefully this unprecedented focus on alternative dispute resolution will eventually lead us to the obvious conclusion that the basic problem may be the manner in which we, as lawyers, sometimes represent our clients in a dispute. The fundamental value of a good lawyer is that he brings not only an expertise in the law but also a detachment and objectivity to a problem which the person involved cannot hope to have, no matter how sophisticated or intelligent. If two good lawyers, faced with a dispute, regardless of complexity, explore the issues from the point of view of achieving a resolution whereby all parties can accept the result then it is surprising how often a fair and expeditious settlement can be achieved. When this occurs, not only has justice been achieved but the lawyers can feel content that they have not only well served their clients but also their profession.

To management theorists ADR may be comprehended as a manifestation of "issues management." But this analysis is best left to those experts. This book attempts to understand ADR in its relationship to litigation and litigants.

As I discussed in Chapter 2, it appears that a consequence of this 'ADR or litigation' approach has been to create a dividing line between two different approaches to dispute resolution. But it's important that we get on one track in our search for justice. "The train is leaving the station," says Norm Bowley, Chairman of the Dispute Resolution Centre of Ottawa-Carleton, to get lawyers involved in ADR. To extend that train metaphor, each car on the train could be symbolic of a different process on the track towards justice. If necessary, passengers will go from car to car until they find one that suits them.

There are many signs that a rift has developed between the two approaches to dispute resolution. For example, in our own community initiatives we have seen that some non-lawyers do not want lawyers involved, and also that some lawyers ignore ADR developments or even hope they will fail. Both are off the track. In the United States, some litigants are justifiably angry at being pointed to as the villains. And finally, some law firms are reluctant to create an ADR department or appoint an ADR coordinator for fear of creating the impression that the firm doesn't already serve its clients' best interests in litigation. For example, the following article appeared in the February 1988 edition of the U.S. newsletter, *Of Counsel: The Legal Practice and Management Report*:

> And Wilbur Boies of Chicago's McDermott, Will & Emery notes that his firm intentionally has avoided establishing an ADR department or otherwise consolidating responsibilities for ADR. That approach, he says, is inconsistent with the firm's strong belief that "these procedures are things all litigators ought to be familiar with, to a greater or lesser extent."
>
> Lapin sounds a similar note. "I don't particularly believe it's a viable approach to the problem to say 'these things are for the lawyers who are going to do ADR,'" he says. "I don't think it really adds anything to segregate it organizationally and give people different hats to wear." That approach may render the ADR "an alien concept" for non-ADR specialists and undercut the message that ADR "is an integral part of our litigation practice—and should be," he suggests. But Lapin endorses the concept of having certain partners serve as a resource for their less knowledgeable or experienced colleagues.

There are many articles and analyses, some dating back to the early 1970s, that discuss the spectrum of dispute resolution options, from negotiation to litigation, or describe three general categories of dispute resolution processes—judicial, quasi-judicial or non-judicial—that can also be combined. Many jurists and academics say the public should have options available to them, and this reasoning includes litigation as one option.

A program proposal prepared by the Ontario Law Reform Commission on Alternative Dispute Resolution in late 1987 astutely identifies this anomaly and notes that "the traditional system of courtroom adjudication is inextricably bound up with the so-called alternative forms of dispute resolution" and that it is "misleading to impose a black and white conceptual distinction between adjudication on one hand and …their variants on the other."

Judge Frank Evans from Texas always reminds lawyers that the court system and enhancements to it are really meant to encourage settlement—indeed, both in the United States and Canada it is accepted that less than 10 per cent of all cases that are instituted end up in trial. In Ontario, many rules of practice are really meant to accelerate the process or encourage settlement (e.g., request to admit, affidavit of documents and certificate, offer to settle, pretrial, trial of an issue, cost penalties to lawyers and parties including the "Torquemada rule," summary judgement, etc.). If these are examples of how one option, litigation, can be improved, then all other options will also need constant improvement, however more suitable they may be for disputants.

Several recent books now advise business people to consider ADR processes as an alternative to litigation; these books, although candid, enlightening and important, fuel the fire that flames the division. Accordingly, before the concept of ADR as an alternative to litigation explodes into the public consciousness, lawyers should carefully think out what's best for the public and consider whether it might not be better to approach their clients with alternatives *for* them and not *from* their lawyers.

Whatever the legitimate historical reasons for the phrase "alternative dispute resolution," its acronym ADR, and its original understanding as an alternative to litigation, perhaps it is a good time to reconsider how we explain the concept to the general public. Mortimer J. Adler's book, *Ten Philosophical Mistakes*, prompted me to wonder whether there needs to be a shift so that ADR is accepted philosophically as an *alternative for people*, and not as an *alternative to litigation*. When I suggested this to Marie Fortier, who practices with Charles Hackland at Lang, Michener and who helped arrange the Carleton Law Association's Annual Litigation Conference, her immediate response was that this approach was more "palatable." Madame Commissioner Maria De Souza, our Family Law Commissioner in Ottawa, seemed to like this approach and asked whether some phrase other than ADR should be considered. My feeling is that it may be easier to maintain the well-known ADR, but simply describe it as an acronym for "alternatives for people." This would be consistent with the writings of many scholars and contemporary jurists, and its ordinary language will resonate with the ordinary person.

The positive nature of this approach also has other benefits:

1. It could avoid the dividing line that we've seen in other jurisdictions between those in ADR and those in litigation;

2. It allows a comprehensible adaptation of the paradigms of dispute resolution as prepared by scholars and jurists, and will be learned by lawyers and other ADR suppliers in the whole range from negotiation to litigation, without an artificial separation of litigation as though it were some stand-alone or 'untouchable' artifact. It may be that litigation will come to be seen as the wild west of dispute resolution. Who knows? Maybe 50 years from now people will be saying: "Why are you mediating? What's the matter? Can't you just talk to one another?" In the meantime, however, no matter how unfortunate it may be, the handshake approach appears more likely to work if the fist is not far away.

3. It clarifies for the public, in plain language, what dispute resolution is all about because the public can see that if litigation is one alternative, there are a whole series of manoeuvres, rules and actions that the courts and lawyers can take on their behalf to achieve what ADR is all about: achieving the most appropriate, fair, efficient and affordable way to resolve the dispute in the search for justice. Accordingly, even within processes other than litigation, internal steps could be taken to continually improve upon and adapt those processes to meet the needs of a case. Some cases may be more appropriate for court adjudication; some cases may be better in a non-court setting, or under the "shadow of the court."

4. It may permit dispute resolution experts who are trial lawyers to work comfortably with other lawyers and non-lawyers who are pursuing other processes to assist people in the resolution of their disputes. Much needs to be done to educate lawyers, judges, and the public at large about these fresh, although not new ideas, to determine which processes are most appropriate, and within those processes, to determine what can be done to satisfactorily resolve these matters. Ultimately, whatever is in the best interest of the client is also in the best interest of both the lawyer and the professional— whatever field that professional is in. Any other considerations are self-serving and in the long run will hurt both the client and the professional.

5. It may help relieve some of the intellectual bickering that is developing between opponents and proponents of ADR. Indeed, to an ordinary person the very debate would seem contradictory or confusing—both sides of the debate either have one thing in common or they do not, i.e., the best interests of the people involved in the dispute. Both sides have good points, but neither is absolutely right or wrong because we're talking about the same issue.

This simple change of explanation is probably no more than an "illuminating glimpse into the obvious," to borrow a phrase from Professor Thomas Feeney, former Dean of the University of Ottawa, Department of Common Law.

In a brief discussion with Dean Peachey, of the Network for Community Justice and Conflict Resolution, he wondered if including litigation in the spectrum of choices might lead to lawyers having an unequal role to play in ADR development. In the true spirit of mediation he said, "Let's talk about it."

But he raises a valid point. It may be said that one underlying reason for the proliferation of non-court processes was to avoid the monopoly that lawyers were perceived to have in dispute resolution. And some are afraid that lawyers will co-opt ADR for purely economic self-interest, thereby creating a malaise with ADR similar to that which now besets the legal system. Any approach that hints at a return to that state of monopoly would, therefore, be anathema to non-lawyers. We would be back to a territorial debate and the disputant may get lost in the shuffle. I suggest that this will not happen, although I concede that the question requires consideration.

Those who have been involved for years will have much to contribute, but my research to date and my instincts suggest that approaching ADR as *alternatives for people* and not *alternatives to litigation* is worth consideration. This is especially so in Canada, where it is generally accepted that we may not be as litigious as our American counterparts. Perhaps the cultural differences between the two countries further justify this shift in interpretation of the nomenclature, although if this proposition finds acceptance with ADR experts in the U.S.A. it would really only follow the lead of Professor Sander over a decade ago. Mr. Justice Linden said in his address to the ABA Special Meeting on Dispute Resolution in January 1987: "Canada is a compromising nation. It is a nation of people who as a society seem more inclined to negotiate and cooperate than to fight."

My only request is that we practise what we preach, and not go to the public in conflict posturing about who has the right answer. The public is subject to enough unnecessary adversarial activity in our society. As for the criticisms levelled against ADR, as one lawyer in a panel said, although the criticism has some merit it is stated with more hyperbole than hostility. In any event, we would do well to remember the saying that "the tall nail on the log always gets hit first!"

All professionals—in every discipline—should collectively seek to find common ground for the best interest of the public that they are privileged to serve. I am wary of the two tendencies that seem to exist in this area. The first tendency is *territorial jealousness,* with various professionals trying to protect their dispute processing area. My position is that no one owns any special turf but we all have a lot to do. The other tendency is toward *messianic zealousness,* and to that I respond that no one has all the answers but each one of us is part of the answer. It would be unfortunate if the public were put in the unenviable position of not only having to seek professional advice on how best to resolve their disputes, but also having to choose between the advice of their litigant and that of other ADR suppliers. This suggested approach might be called too simplistic, but as Judge Evans has pointed out, the area is not that complicated.

Does it make sense to approach ADR as *alternative forms of dispute resolution* (ranging from negotiation to litigation) rather than as *alternative forms of dispute resolution to litigation*? Is it the better way to proceed? Is it understandable to the ordinary citizen? Is it in the best interests of access to justice for the common person?

To help explain ADR and the various processes, a glossary of terms follows. A glossary such as this would be distributed to employees through the proposed *Without Prejudice* program that is discussed in Chapter 5.

GLOSSARY OF TERMS

ACTIVE LISTENING: Making a conscious effort to hear, understand and respond to what is said and felt.

ARBITRATION: Binding settlement of a dispute by an impartial third party (an arbitrator); for example, by a judge or jury

ASSERTIVE: Stating positively but without aggression

BRAINSTORM: To freely share suggestions, inspirations or ideas without discussion or evaluation

COMPROMISE: The process of mutual concession to resolve differences (conflict).

CONFLICT: A problem or disagreement between two or more people; opposition of actions or ideas.

CONFRONT: To face or meet (as a problem); to deal with.

ESCALATION: An increase in the magnitude or intensity; a build up making resolution more difficult.

MEDIATION: A voluntary process for settling disputes in which a neutral third person assists the disputing parties in reaching a mutually beneficial agreement.

NEGOTIATION: Discussion "with a view to reaching agreement"; talking about a conflict where both parties give and take to reach a resolution.

ROLE PLAYING: A learning technique in which two or more people act out characterizations of other people or other communication styles.

VIOLENCE: Force used to injure or take advantage of someone; hurt imposed. Types of violence include physical, verbal, psychological and institutional.

"Dispute Resolution Centre of Ottawa-Carleton, Woodroffe High School Mediation Training Manual, February 1988 (C. Picard, Consultant)

NEGOTIATION: Any form of verbal communication, direct or indirect, whereby parties to a conflict of interest discuss, without resort to arbitration or other judicial processes, the form of any joint action which they might take to manage a dispute between them (1); Communication for the purpose of persuasion (2); Whenever people exchange ideas with the intention of changing relationships, whenever they confer for agreement, they are negotiating (3)

MEDIATION: The intervention of an impartial and neutral third party, who has no decision-making power, into a dispute or negotiation to assist contending parties in reaching a mutually acceptable settlement of issues in dispute (4); A process of conflict resolution in which a neutral third party helps parties in dispute reach a voluntary agreement (5); A process by which disputants attempt to reach a consensual settlement of issues in dispute with the assistance and facilitation of a neutral resource person or persons (6)

ADJUDICATION: A dispute resolution process in which disputants present proofs and arguments to a neutral third party who has the power to hand down a binding decision, generally based on objective standards (7); A formal process in an adversarial setting in which a decision is rendered by a judge based on consideration of evidence and application of law to facts (8); A form of social ordering...in which the relations of men to one another are governed and regulated (9).

From Andrew J. Pirie, *Dispute Regulation in Canada: Present State, Future Direction.*

4 ADR PROCESSES AT WORK

*A good and faithful judge ever prefers
the honorable to the expedient*
–Horace, *Carmina*

In his 1983 Year End Report on the judiciary, former Chief Justice Warren E. Burger urged judges, judicial personnel, legal scholars and the bar to find new ways to cope with the mounting crises in the courts:

> Experimenting with new methods in the judicial system is imperative given growing caseloads, delays, and increasing costs. Federal and state judges throughout the country are trying new approaches to discovery, settlement negotiations, trial and alternatives to trial that deserve commendation and support. The bar should work with judges who are attempting to make practical improvements in the judicial system. Greater efficiency and cost-effectiveness serve both clients and the public. Legal educators and scholars can provide a valuable service by studying new approaches and reporting on successful innovations that can serve as models for other jurisdictions.

The legal community has begun to respond to the chief justice's call for action. This book brings together a number of these innovative responses. It not only presents successful procedures that can serve as models for other jurisdictions, but also advances new ideas for making dispute resolution most cost-effective.

THE ABOVE EXCERPT is the preface to a book by the CPR Legal Program, *ADR and the Courts: A Manual for Judges and Lawyers: Innovative Strategies for Case Management, Early Settlement and Dispute Resolution,* edited by Erika S. Fine and Elizabeth S. Plapinger. Excerpts from this book form the basis of this chapter.

Where noted, this chapter also includes excerpts from another publication, *Manager's Guide to Resolving Legal Disputes: Better Results Without Litigation,* by James F. Henry (President of CPR), and Jethro K. Lieberman.

This chapter provides a quick overview of the main ADR processes, other than litigation, which are addressed in these two publications.

As one comes to understand the nature and depth of the wide opportunities available in the ADR area, one sees it will involve much rewarding work and study. Hence the need for the proposed program, *Without Prejudice* (see Chapter 5), which will be an ongoing educational and information exchange.

OVERVIEW OF PRIVATE ADR PROCESSES

From *ADR and the Courts:*

> Judges and others interested in improving the judicial process are beginning to examine the world of private alternative dispute resolution (ADR) to see how private procedures can be adapted for use in court.
>
> Broadly defined, private ADR encompasses processes for resolving legal disputes outside of court, as well as techniques for managing litigation cost-effectively and preventing litigation from arising in the first place.
>
> The conceptual beginning of the contemporary ADR movement can be dated to 1976, when the American Bar Association convened the Pound Conference, after Roscoe Pound, who in 1906 delivered a talk on the reasons for the public's dissatisfaction with the legal system. At the 1976 conference, Professor Frank E.A. Sander of Harvard Law School delivered his now well-known paper, *Varieties of Dispute Processing*, which reminded the legal community that the traditional court-based process was but one way—albeit an important one—to resolve legal disputes. Sander proposed a multiprocess dispute resolution system that would match different types of disputes to appropriate processes, such as mediation, arbitration, or fact-finding. The Pound Conference led to an interest in ADR among lawyers, judges and legislators, and to an increased use of such alternatives to litigation as mediation in family law matters, misdemeanors, and other small-scale disputes.
>
> The ADR movement also focuses on alternative ways to resolve and reduce the costs of complex, large-scale disputes involving business and public institutions. This area of ADR is the primary focus of [the book, *ADR and the Courts: A Manual for Judges and Lawyers*]. In 1977 the development of a private settlement conference now known as the mini-trial helped encourage the growth of this branch of the ADR movement.

The section below discusses some of the better known ADR processes.

THE MINI-TRIAL

Since the mini-trial is the flagship of ADR processes, I have included material that details its history, features, advantages and disadvantages; other, less commonly used ADR processes are only briefly described. As an aside, in Australia the mini-trial is considered neither a trial nor a mini-trial and is called case assessment.[1]

---

1 Jenny David, Senior Lecturer in Law, University of Sydney, in a seminar, "Are Lawyers Becoming Obsolete as Dispute Resolvers?"

ADR and the Courts includes this description:

Designed by lawyers to untangle years of litigation in a patent case involving TRW and Telecredit, the mini-trial is not actually a trial at all. It is a confidential, non-binding settlement process...

Its creators called it an "information exchange," but it was dubbed a mini-trial in 1978 by a *New York Times* headline writer.

The mini-trial has no fixed form, flexibility being one of its chief advantages. Most mini-trials, however, share certain characteristics. The process is set in motion by an agreement setting forth the ground rules, which often include a limited period of discovery. At the heart of the mini-trial are abbreviated case presentations made by counsel to principals from each side and a neutral advisor of the parties' choosing, often a former judge or an experienced lawyer. If the disputants are corporations the principals are senior executives with settlement authority.

The case presentations enable the executives to gain a clearer view of the strengths and weaknesses of each side's key positions. After the presentations, the executives meet to negotiate settlement. The neutral advisor, if requested, gives an advisory opinion on the likely litigated outcome of the dispute or helps the principals reach agreement.

Most mini-trials result in prompt settlements. The process has been used with particular success in intercorporate disputes. With their knowledge of business operations and objectives, executives are often able to reach innovative resolutions that would be beyond the power of a court to impose, or that lawyers alone would not achieve.

Manager's Guide lists several reasons why mini-trials work, which I have summarized here:

1. the parties negotiate the ground rules;
2. the parties have a limited time to prepare, perhaps six weeks to two months; given this limited time frame the lawyers and the parties are compelled to "suddenly focus on the heart of the matter";
3. "brevity is the soul of the mini-trial" and most range from half a day to two days, depending on complexity;
4. each party must present its "best" case to the executives;
5. the executives are encouraged to settle;
6. a neutral is not always used but experience shows that when a neutral is involved to moderate and conduct, "the mini-trial seems to work best";
7. settlement talks are held immediately by the executives, usually in private except for their lawyers for legal issues, to reduce the settlement to a contract;
8. there is confidentiality, first, because *all* aspects are inadmissible in court in an agreement, subject to relevant jurisprudence in different areas, should

settlement discussions fail, and second, because public discussion of the case is barred.

The origin of the mini-trial is explained in detail in *ADR and the Courts*:

The origin of the mini-trial is explained in detail, involving a six-million-dollar lawsuit between Telecredit Inc., which claimed that giant TRW Inc. was infringing its patent; after two and one-half years, 100,000 documents and no pretrial in sight, the parties wanted a resolution. TRW balked at arbitration for a number of reasons, including whether it could legally be done with a patent case, and to avoid a "split the baby in half" reputation of the arbitrators. Telecredit's co-founder and TRW lawyers worked out an "information exchange" strategy, with six weeks to prepare, four hours to present their "best" case to the other party's top management and senior managers with sides meeting privately often moderated by a "neutral advisor," a respected former patent judge then a practicing lawyer; there was an eight-page set of rules including rebuttals. There were 14 hours of verbal exchange including witnesses. At the end the executives, enlightened because "for the first time in litigation…lawyers divided arguments which sharply pinpointed in their minds in an understandable way each party's precise and factual differences"—they reached a settlement in *thirty minutes,* which was followed within a few weeks by a written legal agreement. The entire process from deciding to make this legal history to signing the agreement was ninety days. Over a million dollars in legal fees were saved, years of time, much court time and management time, and lawyers had satisfied clients. A *New York Times* journalist ran a story on this event coining the word "mini-trial."

Manager's Guide cites seven advantages of a mini-trial:

1. cost reduction
2. creative problem solving
3. preservation of continuing relationship
4. choice of neutral advisor
5. a tailor-made process
6. maintenance of confidentiality
7. dramatic time savings

As a result of these advantages, *Manager's Guide* concludes: "The mini-trial has proved its worth as a practical device of widespread utility."

According to the *Manager's Guide*, deterrents to the mini-trial are:

1. "COUNSEL'S UNFAMILIARITY": A story is told of how Gillette's general counsel, Joseph E. Mulbaney, wished to short-circuit litigation against an ex-employee for trade secret and patent infringement; Mulbaney and the defendant agreed to a mini-trial but Gillette's outside counsel rendered a

memo denouncing the mini-trial and insisting that litigation was the best vehicle. That lawyer was dismissed, another member of the bar was retained who became familiar with and would work with a mini-trial—within six months the mini-trial was held and over lunch the executive settled. "The clear loser," says Mulbaney, "was Gillette's outside lawyer. In opposing the mini-trial idea he argued that the courtroom is the only crucible for getting at the truth." As Mulbaney notes, "That's rather farfetched these days."

2. "TACTICAL USES OF LITIGATION": When looking for a reasonable outcome a mini-trial settlement is preferable to a bitter court fight;

3. "LITIGATION TO DEFER LIABILITY": Dragging out litigation postpones judgement, but with courts awarding interest and penalizing for costs, there should be less persuasion to use this excuse;

4. "LACK OF TRUST": If lawyers or executives don't have a minimum level of trust then perhaps another ADR process could be pursued with a neutral intermediary, such as a structured settlement (i.e., problem solving wherein the parties seek to match their interests, not muscle their rights);

5. "CREDIBILITY OF WITNESS": Some say executives have the savvy and can determine who is lying as well as a jury; a witness not about to tell the truth will likely not be called at a mini-trial;

6. "MISSING EXECUTIVES": In product liability or larger damage claims, there are some questions unresolved, but Union Carbide settled a case with eighteen factory workers by a mini-trial involving a claim for damages from an industrial chemical causing them illness

7. "LARGE OR CRIPPLING JUDGEMENTS": A plaintiff looking for these large awards may be disinterested in a mini-trial, but this may provide an opportunity to encourage more reasonable approaches;

8. "DESIRE FOR A JURY": If this is a compelling deterrent to a plaintiff, it would prevent a mini-trial (but he may be interested in a summary jury trial!);

9. "UNEQUAL BARGAINING POWER": Experience has proved that even when there is unequal bargaining power it is always worth the effort in dollars and money to try a mini-trial anyway;

10. "PURE LEGAL QUESTIONS AS SOLE ISSUES": a respected senior counsel or retired judge could deal with such an issue in a mini-trial as well as in an arbitrary summary judgement procedure, but if a precedent is sought a mini-trial would not be appropriate

MEDIATION

It is generally better to deal by speech than by letter; and by the mediation of a third than by a man's self

—Sir Francis Bacon, *Of Negotiating*

Mediation, centuries old, is receiving renewed attention today and is being called the sleeping giant of business dispute resolution.[2]

Mediation encompasses a variety of techniques, but its defining feature is the use of a third-party neutral who, rather than imposing a solution on the parties, helps them reach their own agreement. The process allows disputing parties to explore settlement possibilities candidly. By learning the confidential concerns and positions of all parties, the mediator can often develop options beyond the perceptions of the disputants.

The mediator's role and the mediation process can take various forms, depending on the nature of the dispute and the relationship of the parties. The mediator can identify and narrow issues, crystallize each side's underlying interests and concerns, carry messages between the parties, explore bases for agreement and the consequences of not settling, and develop a cooperative, problem-solving approach. The mediator may work primarily with lawyers or directly with the disputants themselves. He or she can help the parties fashion their own resolution, or propose a settlement package to them. If they reject the proposed settlement package the mediator can then engage in "shuttle diplomacy," an attempt to bring the parties to an accommodation through a series of separate confidential meetings.

Mediation is frequently used in domestic relations cases and multiparty disputes involving environmental and land use planning issues. Bringing mediation to large-scale disputes involving business and public institutions has been slower. Recently, however, some companies have begun to give mediation a try. For example, in 1985 a thirteen-year-old antitrust case between two New England communications companies was settled through mediation. Called the sleeping giant of private dispute resolution, mediation has the potential for much greater use in the business and institutional context.

CONFIDENTIAL LISTENING

In confidential listening, a quick, risk-free process, parties submit their confidential settlement positions to a third-party neutral who then informs them whether their positions are within a negotiable range. The neutral or confidential listener does not relay one side's confidential offer to the other.

The ground rules of the procedure are fixed before settlement positions are exchanged and, as in all private processes, may vary according to the needs of the

---

2 Some commentators are calling for "full-fledged professionals" or Certified Professional Mediators (CPMs); it is predicted that the ironic, and to some, entertaining day will come when mediators and other third-party neutrals will themselves be defendants in malpractice lawsuits. One pointed criticism by Crouch is useful to remember: "Mediation is not the cure-all that the hucksters, the cultists and happy zealots among the learned professions would have us believe, but it is a worthwhile idea. If mediation lowers (costs)…and gives people settlements that they are more willing to live with because they can't blame the mistakes on their lawyers, then it will be a noble achievement."

parties and the character of the dispute. For example, the parties may agree that if the proposed settlement figures overlap, with the plaintiff citing a lower figure, they will settle at a level that splits the difference. If the proposed figures are within a specified range of each other, e.g., ten percent, the parties may direct the neutral to so inform them and help them negotiate to narrow the gap. And if the submitted numbers are not within the set range, the parties might repeat the process.

This privately developed device provides a simple way to circumvent the widespread reluctance of counsel to disclose their realistic settlement positions early in a dispute. Its users have also commented that the simple act of estimating the value of a claim may reorient the disputants towards settlement.

NEUTRAL FACT-FINDING

In this process, a third-party neutral with substantive or technical expertise examines and evaluates disputed facts central to the controversy. The fact-finder, who is not authorized to resolve the matter, then submits a report detailing his or her findings. Such information may reduce uncertainty and thus promote settlement.

NEGOTIATION

Negotiation, the mainstay of dispute resolution, has also come under scrutiny recently to improve the quality of negotiated legal outcomes.

Legal academics are studying lawyers' negotiation behavior and exploring ways parties can become more effective negotiators. One major emphasis of the developing negotiation literature, as chronicled by Professor Carrie Menkel-Meadow in "Legal Negotiation" (1983 *Am. B. Found. Research J.* 905) is that good negotiators will look beyond the stated positions of the parties to the concerns and interests they are trying to protect or develop. Lawyers are being urged to approach negotiation as creative problem-solvers who can broaden the range of possible solutions.

One consequence of the new negotiation theory and research has been the separation of the litigation and negotiation functions. Two "teams" have been used to resolve disputes, one consisting of negotiators and the other of litigators, so that lawyers uninvolved in litigation can conduct settlement talks.

One commentator has suggested that one of the earliest and best examples of a negotiation is found in Genesis 18:20-33, where a colloquy is reported to have taken place between the Lord and Abraham. In this passage the Lord says He will destroy the sinful cities of Sodom and Gomorrah but Abraham tries to save Sodom, the home of his nephew Lot, by negotiating with God. If 50 righteous people can be found among the wicked, Abraham says to God, will you save the city? God agrees, but Abraham keeps negotiating down—from 50 righteous people to 45, 40, 30, 20, and finally 10. Apparently those 10 righteous people could not be found, for the cities of Sodom and Gomorrah are destroyed but Lot and his family escape.

ARBITRATION

Long used to resolve commercial and labor disputes, arbitration involves a neutral who hears each side's case and then imposes a final and binding decision on the parties. Arbitration awards are enforceable by the courts, and can only be set aside under highly unusual circumstances, such as fraud. Arbitration is often agreed to in a contract as a way to resolve future disputes arising out of the contract.

Despite its potential for speed, low cost and informality, arbitration has been criticized for being increasingly slow, expensive and formal. In addition, arbitrators have been criticized for their tendency to compromise or "split the baby" rather than reach well-grounded decisions.

Special arbitration techniques are being created to prevent the rigidities that sometimes characterize conventional arbitration. One example is "final-offer" arbitration. The parties each submit a proposed award to the arbitrator, who must choose one or the other without modification or compromise. Because an extreme position will usually lead the arbitrator to choose the other, the incentive for the parties is to negotiate a solution before submission to the arbitrator and, failing that, to provide the arbitrator with a proposal that is not extreme.

Another variation is nonbinding arbitration. Although arbitration traditionally is binding, parties can agree that the neutral's opinion will be advisory only. Even though advisory, the opinion is likely to carry great weight in the parties' subsequent settlement discussion.

PRIVATE TRIALS

Parties can agree on their own, without court involvement, to select a private "judge"—perhaps a highly experienced neutral attorney or former federal or state judge—and conduct a private trial under their own rules. Such proceedings can be party-directed, or they can rely on strong assistance from the neutral. They may have the informality of non-binding procedures like the mini-trial or they may parallel traditional court processes and retain certain procedural or evidentiary rules. Parties may want the private judge to provide the same sort of well-grounded opinion they would receive in a bench trial.

In some states, private trials can take place under a reference statute. Under these statutes, the court, upon agreement by the parties, can appoint a "referee" or "private judge" to resolve the dispute. Procedurally, the private trial is flexible, but in general, the proceedings are conducted in much the same manner as a bench trial, although in an expedited and simplified manner. Unlike an arbitration award, the decision of a referee can be appealed.

In Toronto we have seen the recent development of the private court (see Chapter 7). There is also the well-known variant of arbitrating "trial by reference," or as the *Wall Street Journal* has dubbed it, trial by "rent-a-judge."

NEW DEVELOPMENTS

An advantage of ADR is its flexibility. Creative lawyers are developing new ADR procedures—often by combining or adapting those described above—to suit the needs of particular parties or certain types of cases.

The CPR Legal Program, a nonprofit coalition of leading attorneys from major companies, law firms and law schools, develops new procedures for specific types of disputes, such as product liability, employment, transnational, technology, and hazardous waste cases. In CPR's procedure for personal-injury product-liability cases, for example, attorneys for each side present their cases to a mutually select- ed neutral. The neutral then makes a reasoned, non-binding determination of the settlement value of the claim. In some cases, parties may want to accept the neu- tral's determination. If they do not, it becomes the basis for settlement negotiations, which, under the procedure, the parties have agreed to conduct. (The product lia- bility procedure and others developed by the CPR Legal Program are available from the Center for Public Resources in New York City.)

LITIGATION MANAGEMENT

Proponents of private ADR do not believe all disputes can or even should be resolved out of court. For disputes that do end up in court, the ADR movement aims to reduce litigation costs by injecting managerial techniques into the practice of law.

In recent years, various techniques have emerged to help law firms, compa- nies and other institutions manage litigation better. Two of these processes are the litigation budget and litigation risk analysis. Both help lawyers and their clients analyze the financial and strategic consequences of their litigation decisions.

The litigation budget is a financial plan developed by counsel at the outset of a dispute and periodically updated. The budget identifies and allocates funds for the multiplicity of tasks involved in litigation, such as legal research and specific aspects of discovery. The budgeting process forces both counsel and client to think hard about the steps to be taken in a particular dispute, the costs associated with each, and the likely returns from expenditures. It helps ensure cost-effective professional judgements at each stage of litigation. In addition, it enables lawyer and client to discuss the financial implications of the dispute openly, early and continually. Even if the dollar amounts are imprecise, budgeting can be useful for projecting and con- trolling costs, identifying alternatives to litigation, coordinating the efforts of inside and outside counsel, and preparing detailed plans to show goals, staffing and deadlines.

Litigation risk analysis is a quasi-mathematical process that helps lawyers and managers decide whether and how to proceed with litigation or its alternatives. The process allows counsel to evaluate systematically the probable outcomes of key lit- igation decisions and factor these assessments into a decision tree, a chart that schemat- ically forecasts the dispute's overall value and the chances of success. Risk analysis imposes a discipline on the traditionally unstructured processes of litigation planning and evaluation of settlement options. In addition, it enhances communication between counsel and client by providing them with a common frame of reference.

Litigation risk analysis and litigation budgeting combine lawyering skills and business skills. This reflects a larger ADR theme: greater involvement of business managers (or clients) in the way that law is practiced on their behalf. This development is altering the traditional lawyer-client business relationship and promoting a variety of innovative, cost-effective dispute management techniques.

These techniques include letters outlining the company's litigation policy to newly retained firms; careful scrutiny of bills from outside counsel; new billing techniques; increased coordination of inside and outside counsel to share litigation tasks cost-effectively; and, in general, greater supervision by the client company of the litigation process.

Just as participation of management representatives is critical to the success of dispute resolution processes like the mini-trial, the client's knowledge of the company's underlying interests and business concerns is essential to better litigation management. Early involvement of executives helps set corporate objectives, determines what course to follow, permits a narrowing of the scope of the dispute, and brings the manager into the process as ally and participant.

Companies and laws firms are also restructuring their internal legal resources to promote ADR and better dispute management. One law firm, for example, has created a special Negotiation-Dispute Resolution Department. Attorneys from this department explore settlement and other ADR options with the firm's litigators, clients and perhaps opposing counsel. Other firms have designated one attorney as an ADR expert to keep up-to-date on developments in the field and discuss ADR options with litigators. These strategies are designed to overcome assumptions that prevent or postpone settlement. Similarly, at least one company now calls its litigation department the "Dispute Resolution Department" to encourage attorneys to consider alternatives to litigation.

Complex multiparty cases—now a familiar part of the litigation landscape—have also spurred the development of new case management strategies. Co-parties with similar interests are now cooperating to streamline litigation. These cooperative strategies include sharing counsel for specific tasks or the entire litigation, common data management and document centers, and agreements among defendants to share litigation costs and allocate damages.

DISPUTE PREVENTION

Another aim of ADR is preventive—to anticipate and avoid future legal problems, or, if unavoidable, plan for their effective private resolution. Companies or other organizations have implemented a range of preventive practices, some directed at altering institutional practices that may invite litigation, and others designed to structure outside business relationships to provide for the sound treatment of future disputes.

Two related practices—compliance programs and legal audits—are finding increasing use among major corporations and other large institutions. The goal of both devices is to alter the day-to-day conduct of the organization in order to minimize the possibility of future litigation.

In compliance programs, key employees are taught the nature of critical legal and regulatory requirements and the dangers of their violation. Compliance programs have been used to monitor and ensure organizational compliance with environmental, securities, employment and antitrust laws.

The legal audit, also known as a legal review or check-up, is a planning device. A close examination of an organization's business activities and legal affairs, the legal audit is designed to predict potential legal disputes and identify ways current activities and practices can be changed to reduce risks.

Companies have also developed system-wide preventive programs for specific substantive areas. In the product liability area, preventive programs combine legal, business and engineering expertise at various operational phases, such as product design and the development of instructions and warnings, with the goal of avoiding future litigation and liability.

In the employment area, companies and other organizations are reducing or eliminating litigation by using in-house neutrals, or ombudsmen, to investigate complaints and mediate to detect incipient problems within the organization and address them early through policy change or otherwise.

In addition to altering internal practices to anticipate and avoid needless litigation, organizations are beginning to structure their external business affairs to avoid the escalation of disputes into lawsuits. Two major kinds of preventive initiatives are underway in this area.

One is the Corporate Policy Statement on ADR, which has been signed by over 200 major corporations since its issuance in 1984 by the Center for Public Resources. Through the Policy Statement, a company declares that it will explore ADR techniques in future disputes with other signers. The aim of the Policy—and its effect thus far—is to overcome corporate reliance on litigation by making it easier to initiate ADR or even early settlement discussions.

A second and complementary way to plan for future dispute resolution is by contract. During contract formation, negotiating parties are addressing possible future disputes through use of dispute resolution clauses. Inclusion of these clauses can curb the reflexive initiation at the point of dispute.

Creative lawyering in recent years has considerably broadened the range of alternatives for the contract drafter. Mediation, mini-trial and other ADR clauses are now being included in contracts, in addition to boilerplate arbitration clauses. In some ADR clauses parties incorporate by reference specific alternative procedures (such as the mini-trial) and then modify the selected procedure at the point of dispute to fit their needs. In other contracts, parties negotiate detailed dispute resolution provisions.

The enforceability of clauses providing for nonbinding ADR is unclear. Some commentators, relying on strict contract doctrine, argue against specific enforceability because the clauses do not obligate either party to convey an ultimate benefit on the other. Others cite the federal and state doctrines favoring settlement to predict enforceability. Still another group insists that the question is largely irrelevant, arguing that most well-drafted ADR clauses will provide for good faith participation in ADR as a condition precedent to litigation and that even the most litigation-prone party will have an interest in establishing his good faith.

United States District Chief Judge Jack B. Weinstein, in a case of first impression, recently enforced an agreement between two manufacturers to engage in private, nonbinding ADR, holding that the contested dispute resolution contract clauses (1) constituted an enforceable agreement to arbitrate under the Federal Arbitration Act, and alternatively (2) were specifically enforceable because the plaintiff did not have adequate remedy at law. *AMF Inc. v. Brunswick Corp.*, 621 F. Supp. 456 (E.D.N.Y. 1985)

In his opinion, Judge Weinstein strongly approved the use of ADR procedures: "General public policy favors support to alternatives to litigation when these alternatives serve the interests of the parties and of judicial administration. Here (the parties)…agreed…that a special ADR mechanism would serve them better than litigation."

CONCLUSION: PRIVATE ADR

This discussion of private ADR—ways to solve, manage, and prevent disputes—is not exhaustive. Inventive attorneys are continually adapting these techniques and developing new ones to address the variety of problems they encounter in their practices.

Some of these private processes, such as arbitration, mediation and the mini-trial, have been translated by judges lawyers, and policymakers for use in court. It is hoped that this overview of private ADR will inspire further creative adaptations. In addition, the overview should encourage judges through Rule 16(c)(7) of the Federal Rules of Civil Procedure, to explore "use of extrajudicial procedures" and recommend these and other ADR processes in appropriate cases.

One example of creative problem solving was described at a seminar by Judge Frank Evans, who talked about an ADR process at his Court of Appeal in Texas. Appellate lawyers were invited to voluntarily undergo some mediation training and case assessment panels were set up for appeals. As a result, about 10 per cent of the court load was reduced. But as Judge Evans noted, if the Court has 800 appeals and even 10 per cent or 80 of them are settled, that amounts to a substantial savings in time and money for the Court. Reaction to this program was favourable; one participant wrote on the evaluation: "too bad we couldn't do this six or seven years ago."

A second example is an article in the Hartford *Courant* newspaper in Massachusetts, in which the headline read: "Mediators work out $41 million...settlement." The article dealt with the L'Ambiance Plaza collapse of April 1987. With almost 100 party litigants, including more than 40 defendants, a panel of judges acting as mediators with senior counsel appointed as special masters and all parties represented by attorneys, most issues were settled through negotiation and mediation within two years!

And yet a third example of creative problem solving is one that was recounted by author William F. Buckley, Jr. in his book, *Overdrive: A Personal Documentary*. Mr. Buckley, who had brought a libel action against Macmillan Publishing Company, explained how he and the president of Macmillan met for breakfast during the trial, which had gotten out of hand. Within 45 minutes both parties agreed to a $50,000 settlement. Wanting to protect its reputation, MacMillan did not want to pay Mr. Buckley so instead it bought advertising worth $50,000 in Mr. Buckley's magazine, *National Review*. As part of the deal, a year later Macmillan published Mr. Buckley's next book, *Airborne*, and gave the first $50,000 that the book earned to Mr. Buckley to pay for the ads. So, when the protagonists are frustrated with the time and cost involved in the legal system, which only has a restricted array of remedies for litigants, they will come up with very creative business solutions that fit their idiosyncrasies.

Some Model Dispute Resolution Clauses

ARBITRATORS' INSTITUTE OF CANADA, STANDARD ARBITRATION CLAUSE

"All disputes or differences arising in regard to this contract shall be settled by arbitration in accordance with the Rules for the Conduct of Arbitrations of the Arbitrators' Institute of Canada Inc. in effect at the date of commencement of such arbitration, by ( ) arbitrators appointed in accordance with the said rules. The arbitrations will take place in the City of __ unless otherwise agreed and will be final and binding. The law governing the procedures and substance of the arbitration will be..."

The following model clauses are excerpted from *Dispute Resolution* by Stephen B. Goldberg, Eric D. Green and Frank E.A. Sander:

AMERICAN ARBITRATION ASSOCIATION STANDARD ARBITRATION CLAUSE

Any controversy or claim arising out of or relating to this contract, or the breach thereof, shall be settled by arbitration in accordance with the Commercial Arbitration Rules of the American Arbitration Association, and judgment upon the award rendered may be entered in any Court having jurisdiction thereof.

MODEL MEDIATION CLAUSE

The parties shall meet, negotiate in good faith and attempt to resolve amicably, without litigation, any controversy or claim arising out of or relating to this contract, or the breach thereof. If the parties are unable to resolve the matter themselves, they will participate in mediation [with a mutually acceptable third party.] or [The mediator shall be ....] or [The mediation shall be conducted under the auspices of ....]

MODEL MINI-TRIAL DISPUTE RESOLUTION CLAUSE

1. If a dispute arises under the Agreement which cannot be resolved by the personnel directly involved, either party may invoke this dispute resolution procedure by giving written notice to the other designating a senior executive officer with appropriate authority to be its representative in negotiations relating to the dispute.

2. Upon receipt of the notice, the other party shall, within five business days, designate a senior executive officer with similar authority to be its representative.

3. Within 10 business days of the designation of both executives, the designated executives shall enter into direct good faith negotiation concerning the dispute.

4. If the dispute is not resolved as a result of such discussions, at the request of their executive the parties shall engage in a mini-trial as generally described in "The CPR Mini-Trial Handbook."

5. Upon such request for a mini-trial, counsel for the parties shall communicate concerning the ground rules and a schedule for the conduct of the mini-trial, including the selection and compensation of the Neutral Advisor (if any), and a procedure and schedule for exchange of documents and other information related to the dispute.

6. Following the conclusion of the mini-trial, the executives shall continue direct contacts and attempt to resolve the dispute.

7. Neither party may commence litigation or file for arbitration of any dispute under the Agreement until sixty (60) days after completion of the mini-trial except for good cause shown and providing it has made a good-faith effort to comply with all provisions of this clause.

JOINT VENTURE DISPUTE RESOLUTION PROCEDURE: NEGOTIATION, COOLING-OFF, MINI-TRIAL, AND LEAST-FAVOURED LITIGATION FORUM

Dispute Resolution Clause: In the event of any dispute or disagreement among the Parties as to any provision of this Agreement (including any provision of any Schedule, Exhibit or Related Agreement) and, without limiting the generality of the foregoing, any dispute relating to the Joint Venture, upon the written request of any Party, the matter shall immediately be referred jointly to senior management of each party. Such managers shall meet immediately and attempt in good faith to negotiate a resolution of the dispute.

If they do not agree upon a decision within thirty (30) days after reference of the matter to them, any Party may within thirty (30) days, after the thirty (30) days first referenced above, elect to utilize a mini-trial whereby each Party presents its case at a hearing before a panel consisting of a senior executive of each Party and a mutually acceptable Neutral Advisor. The parties may be represented at the mini-trial by lawyers. Prior to the mini-trial the Parties shall meet to mutually agree on a set of ground rules for the mini-trial and a site therefore. In the event the Parties cannot reasonably promptly agree on the ground rules, Neutral Advisor or hearing site, or any of the foregoing, if the Party initiating this dispute resolution procedure is *X* (foreign company), the [Country] Consul General in its capital city, or whatever official is then exercising the powers and authority of such Consul General, shall designate the ground rules, Neutral Advisor or site, and if the Party initiating this dispute resolution procedure is *Y* ([Domestic] Company) the Consul General in the foreign company's capital city, or whatever official is then exercising the powers and authority of such Consul General, shall designate the ground rules, Neutral Advisor or site. At the conclusion of the mini-trial, the Parties' senior executives shall meet and attempt to resolve the matter. If the matter cannot be resolved at such meeting, the Neutral Advisor may be called upon by either executive to render his opinion as to how the matter would be resolved had the hearing been a trial in a court of law. After the opinion is received, the senior executives shall meet and try again to resolve the matter. If the matter cannot be resolved at such meeting, either Party may give the other Party notice of its intention to litigate.

No litigation may commence concerning the matter in dispute until sixty (60) days have elapsed from the sending of the notice of intention to litigate. Any litigation must be filed in the country of the opposing party. The Parties shall bear their respective costs incurred in connection with this procedure, except that the Parties shall share, in proportion to their ownership interests in the Joint Venture, the fees and expenses of the Neutral Advisor, the costs of the facility for the mini-trial, and fee or charge, if any, of the applicable Consul General.

SEMI-BINDING FORUMS

Great cases like hard cases make bad law

—Oliver Wendell Holmes, Jr., *Northern Securities Co.* v. *United States*

A number of courts have created alternative forums for hearing and resolving disputes. Typically, these forums remove cases, at least temporarily, from the court's docket. They are "semi-binding" because parties incur penalties if they reject the award or decision of the alternative forum and do not obtain a better result at trial.

COURT-ANNEXED ARBITRATION

The most common alternative forum is a court-annexed arbitration, which, unlike its private commercial counterpart, is neither voluntary nor binding. Typically, court-annexed arbitration is mandatory for money damage suits—essentially, personal injury, property damage, or contract cases—in which no more than a certain amount is demanded.

In the arbitration hearing, counsel make abbreviated case presentations to a panel of lawyers serving as arbitrators, who then render an award. To preserve the right to jury trial, the award is not binding. However, the award is entered as a judgment of the court unless a party, within a prescribed time period, rejects the award and files a demand for a trial *de novo*. The party demanding trial is subject to a penalty—imposition of costs or arbitration fees—if it fails to improve its position at the subsequent trial.

As Deborah Hensler (The Institute for Civil Justice, The Rand Corporation) points out [elsewhere in the book, *ADR and the Courts*] the process originated and is still most common in the state trial courts. Recently, however, a number of federal courts have instituted arbitration programs.

Hensler reviews a number of studies of court-annexed arbitration. In general, the studies show that court-annexed arbitration has the potential to reduce court congestion, court costs, time to disposition, and costs to litigants, but whether arbitration actually achieves these goals depends on the operational details of the individual program, the number of requests for trial *de novo*, and various other factors.

MICHIGAN "MEDIATION" OR VALUATION

As U.S. District Judge Richard A. Enslen (Western District of Michigan) explains in his chapter on Michigan "Mediation," the procedure, despite its name, does not involve true mediation. Instead of facilitating settlement the three-person mediation panel makes a valuation of the case after hearing brief presentations by counsel.

As in court-annexed arbitration, if the valuation or award is not rejected by either party within a prescribed time period, it is entered as a judgment of the court. If the mediation panel's valuation is unanimous and the valuation is rejected, penalties are imposed on the rejecting party if it does not better the valuation by more than ten percent at trial.

Michigan Mediation began in the state trial court in Wayne County (Detroit) and later was adopted by Michigan's federal courts. In the federal program, cases are referred to mediation by stipulation of the parties, by motion of one party with notice to the other, or on the court's own motion. Most cases assigned to mediation in Judge Enslen's district are on the court's order. All civil cases in his district are eligible for mediation, except those involving constitutional rights.

The program has been successful in expediting disposition of cases and relieving court congestion. In addition, the process seems to facilitate settlement. Some cases are settled even before the mediation process begins. Apparently, simply setting a case for a mediation hearing forces lawyers to evaluate their cases and focus on settlement possibilities. Other cases are settled after rejection of the mediators' valuation, but before trial.

SETTLEMENT STRATEGIES

Courts can use a number of devices to facilitate early settlement. Unlike the procedures described in [Semi Binding Forums], those discussed here emphasize settlement discussions between the parties rather than a decision or valuation (albeit a "semi-binding" one) by a third-party neutral. The settlement discussions can be facilitated by a neutral, perhaps an attorney-mediator, or by the input of an advisory jury. Participation by clients, not just lawyers, is important to most of these settlement strategies. Most do not involve any sort of penalty for inability to settle; the case simply proceeds to trial; however, parties do risk substantial penalties if they fail to reach settlement within a certain time period and reject the neutral's subsequent recommendation.

Courts can also use special masters to mediate or facilitate settlement, particularly in complex cases. (See Judicial Adjuncts.)

SETTLEMENT HEARINGS: SUMMARY JURY TRIAL

One way to facilitate settlement is to remove one of its most common barriers: uncertainty about how a jury will react to evidence presented at trial. The summary jury trial (SJT) was designed by U.S. District Judge Thomas D. Lambros (Northern District of Ohio) to do exactly that.

The SJT gives attorneys and clients the opportunity to see how a jury responds to their case. Because it is non-binding, it does not impair the constitutional right to a jury trial. However, a full jury trial is usually unnecessary because parties are able to settle their case after the SJT.

Summary jury trial is used in "hard core" cases that have not settled through conventional pre-trial procedures. It is most beneficial when a case is ready for trial, with discovery completed and no motions pending. The process has been used in a wide range of cases, from simple negligence and contract actions to complex antitrust and toxic tort matters.

An SJT typically consists of a half-day proceeding in which a judge or magistrate presides. Principals with authority to negotiate settlement are required to attend. Counsel usually have one hour each to present their cases to the jury, although time allotments can be extended if the case is unusually complex.

After the presentations, the jury receives an abbreviated charge and retires for deliberation. Unanimous verdicts are encouraged, but jurors are permitted to return with individual verdicts.

In some cases, parties reach settlement during or immediately after the SJT. Often, however, it takes several weeks for the parties to assess the impact of the SJT verdict. In such cases, a settlement conference should be scheduled a few weeks after the summary jury trial. The SJT result provides an objective basis for settlement discussions that did not exist at the time of the impasses preceding the SJT.

The SJT has proven to be effective in producing settlements. It has spread beyond Judge Lambro's federal court in Ohio to federal and state courts throughout the country. The procedure is flexible; judges have modified it to meet unique needs of jurisdictions or cases.

COURT-SUPERVISED MINI-TRIAL IN MASSACHUSETTS

Another type of settlement hearing is the conditional summary trial of court-supervised mini-trial, which has been used by U.S. District Judge Robert E. Keeton (District of Massachusetts) to, among other things, resolve a complex, seven-year-old lawsuit.

In some respects, the conditional summary trial is similar to the private mini-trial. (See Overview of Private ADR, above). Both involve limited discovery periods followed by abbreviated case presentations made to principals with settlement authority, and both culminate in settlement negotiations between the principals. In Judge Keeton's conditional summary trials, however, there are strong inducements to early settlement. A judicial officer—judge, magistrate, or special master—presides over the hearing, and significant monetary sanctions are imposed on a party who rejects settlement and fails to better the officer's recommended disposition at a subsequent trial.

Although the details of the procedure depend on the individual case, each party generally has about five hours for its presentation, including opening statement, affirmative case, rebuttal, questioning and summation. The time allotted for negotiations between business representatives is also limited, perhaps to a few hours or a full day. The executives may negotiate on their own or with the presiding officer's assistance. If they fail to reach agreement within the prescribed time period, the presiding officer recommends a disposition. In some cases, the disposition is wholly fashioned by the officer, based on his or her views of the strengths and weaknesses of the parties' positions. In others, the business representatives each file a proposed disposition and the neutral must choose between them. (This version of the process resembles final-offer arbitration. See Section I: Overview of Private ADR.) Either way, the officer's recommendation becomes the judgment unless a party files a timely written objection and posts an appropriate bond. By continuing to litigate, the objecting party incurs a substantial penalty—as much as $250,000 payable to the other party—if the litigated outcome is not more favorable to it than the disposition proposed or selected by the presiding officer.

In short, the conditional summary trial or court-supervised mini-trial, as conceived by Judge Keeton, adds bite and structure to the private mini-trial. One virtue of the procedure, according to Judge Keeton, is its ability to prod parties into making genuine, "best" or "final" proposals early in the suit, rather than after expensive, extensive trial preparation.

MEDIATION

A number of courts have created mediation programs to aid the settlement process. In many respects, mediation is a traditional judicial tool. In talking to parties at pre-trial or special settlement conferences, judges often play mediating roles. Sometimes a judge not assigned to the case acts as mediator in the settlement conference. (See e.g., N.D. Cal. Local Rule 240.) If the parties know that a settlement judge will not preside at a trial if the case is not settled, they may be more candid during the settlement conference.

In recent years, courts have begun to use mediation in new, innovative ways. Some courts are involving people from outside the court as paid or volunteer mediators, either in formal programs or on an ad hoc basis. The mediators may serve as Rule 53 (Fed. R. Civ.P.) special masters. Typically they are lawyers, law professors or retired judges from the community.

Some mediation programs, such as the one in the U.S. District Court for the Western District of Washington, are designed to help relieve pressure on judicial caseloads. Others are intended to give parties the opportunity to explore settlement with a third-party neutral who may have certain qualities that a judge, because of his position, lacks. For example, a private attorney serving as mediator may have greater expertise in the area of law at issue in the dispute. The attorney may also have the flexibility to devote large blocks of time to the case, or to design a process tailored to the parties' needs. (For a discussion of Rule 53 special masters as mediators, see Judicial Adjuncts.)

VOLUNTEER ATTORNEY MEDIATION IN WASHINGTON

In his chapter [in the book *ADR and the Courts*] District Judge John C. Coughenour describes the operation of Local Civil Rule 39.1 in the Western District of Washington. Under the rule, judges in the district are authorized to maintain a register of experienced attorneys available to service as volunteer mediators on civil cases. (A similar rule has been adopted by the Eastern Districts of Washington.)

Referral of a case to mediation is discretionary with the judge. Often the court will consult with counsel in determining whether mediation is appropriate. One judge prefers referring cases to mediation soon after the complaint is filed; others refer cases when discovery is substantially completed. The timing of the referral may also depend on the size and complexity of the case.

Once the judge designates a case for mediation, the parties must engage in at least one settlement conference on their own, without a mediator. If the parties are unable to reach settlement at the conference, they select a mediator. In the rare cases in which counsel cannot agree on a mediator, the court designates one.

The attorney primarily responsible for the case must attend the mediation conference. Clients must be available, but the mediator decides whether they actually attend the conference. (They usually do.) The mediation process itself varies from case to case, depending on the style of the mediator, the nature of the case, the attitude of parties and counsel, and the timing of mediation. The mediation proceedings are privileged and confidential.

The judges in the Western District of Washington all believe that volunteer attorney mediation is a useful case management device. The local federal bar association, which administers the program, is also enthusiastic, and has even recommended that all civil cases be referred to mediation.

MEDIATION IN KANSAS FEDERAL COURT

The federal court in Wichita, Kansas also has a panel of lawyers available to serve as mediators. The Kansas panel consists of forty-five attorneys with good reputations and at least ten years' civil trial experience. Unlike the volunteer mediators in Washington, those in Wichita are paid for their services, at a rate of $100 per hour.

Governing the program is Local Rule 45, which gives Kansas federal judges the authority to assign any civil case to another judge, a magistrate, or, with the parties' consent, an attorney-mediator, for a frank informal discussion of settlement prospects. The rule is mandatory in the sense that a judge can require parties to engage in the conference. The parties' consent, however, is necessary if one of the attorney-mediators is to handle the case because parties must pay the chosen attorney-mediator a fee.

In the conference, which typically takes half a day but may last up to three days in a complex matter, the lawyers make brief initial statements of their positions. Clients with settlement authority are required to attend. The mediator often meets privately with each side, candidly evaluating the case, narrowing issues and probing for the basis of an accord.

Although the mediators often play a very active role, the conferences are not coercive in any way. Parties who do not settle simply proceed to trial, with no sanctions. The mediation proceedings are entirely confidential.

Scheduling the conference early in the case is one clue to the program's success. Some cases are settled before the conference even takes place; simply setting a date seems to encourage serious exploration of settlement.

U.S. District Judge Patrick F. Kelly, chief architect of the program, reports that mediation has resulted in settlement in a wide variety of cases, particularly in complex matters. In addition, attorneys who have participated in the program strongly favor it.

EARLY DISPOSITION STRATEGIES

Early dispositions strategies are designed to help parties confront and fully understand their cases earlier than they normally do. By focusing on cases earlier, rational discovery plans can be developed, the pre-trial process can be abbreviated, and earlier settlement can result.

Early disposition procedures may involve assistance from a non-judge neutral advisor (for example, a private attorney) who evaluates the case or recommends discovery or motion plans. Or the court can require parties, on their own, to attempt in good faith to develop a minimum discovery plan. The court can also invite parties to make a minimum summary judgment or other motions to help define and streamline the case early on.

EARLY NEUTRAL EVALUATION

The overriding purpose of the early neutral evaluation project in the San Francisco federal court is to make litigation less expensive for litigants. The program responds to several problems that lead to unnecessary cost and delay: failure of lawyers and clients to assess their cases early, uncommunicative pleadings, and unnecessary or unfocused discovery.

The central feature of the program is a confidential two-hour evaluation conference that takes place early in litigation. The session is conducted by a neutral, highly respected attorney appointed by the court as a special master. Each side, in the presence of its opponent, presents its case to the neutral, who then helps the parties find areas of agreement and identify the core issues in dispute. The neutral next assesses each side's case and makes a valuation. If appropriate, the evaluator helps the parties devise a plan for discovery for motions to generate additional information needed for serious settlement discussions. The evaluator's assessment and valuation are confidential and cannot be shared with the court.

In short, the program is designed to improve the quality and speed of dispute resolution by forcing parties to focus on their cases early in the lawsuit. The neutral, through his or her case evaluation and recommendations regarding discovery and motions, can materially facilitate settlement.

PROPOSAL FOR ABBREVIATING COMPLEX CASES

Gerald Sobel's (Kaye, Scholer, Fierman, Hays, & Handler) proposal for abbreviating complex cases involves a discovery period limited in scope and time, followed by a settlement or ADR procedure. Sobel recognizes that settlement becomes practical when parties fully understand their cases. Like the early neutral evaluation program, Sobel's proposal is designed to make parties analyze and assess their cases earlier than they otherwise would.

Sobel suggests that parties try to develop an abbreviated discovery plan and brief what they cannot agree on to the court. To assist judges, model minimum document requests and interrogatories would be available in a range of substantive areas, such as antitrust, patent infringement, and toxic torts. Additional pinpointed discovery could be allowed within a "substantial need" standard, a more restrictive test than that allowed under Federal Rule of Civil Procedure 26.

If resolution of a contested rule of law or partial summary judgment would have great impact on the claimed recovery, the court should invite appropriate motions and decide them. Following the minimum discovery period and decisions on motions, the parties would submit short briefs to the court. At this time, they would also define the additional discovery needed to prepare for a full trial on the merits. After reviewing the briefs, the judge would attempt to settle the case at a pre-trial conference. If that effort fails, or as an alternative, the court should refer the case to a mini-trial or other non-binding alternative dispute resolution forum. If the case still cannot be settled, the scope of additional discovery needed to prepare for trial should be addressed by the court, based on the request previously submitted. Because the proposed procedure does not foreclose full discovery and trial if settlement is not achieved, it does not abridge any right to discovery or full trial.

JUDICIAL ADJUNCTS: SPECIAL MASTERS AND COURT-APPOINTED EXPERTS

Rule 53 of the Federal Rules of Civil Procedure (special masters) and Rule 706 of the Federal Rules of Evidence (court-appointed experts) provide judges with two vehicles for managing and facilitating settlement in complex cases.

Special masters have long been used by courts, but in recent years, courts have begun to employ them in new, innovative ways, particularly in complex litigation. The roles of special masters can be divided into three broad categories:

1. *Fact-finding.* The traditional special master role under Rule 53, fact-finding, involves helping the judge ascertain the facts at the trial stage, or helping the jury unravel a complicated set of facts.
2. *Discovery/Case Management.* This category can be viewed as a spectrum, ranging from managing specific discovery tasks to overseeing the whole pre-trial development of a case or a series of cases.
3. *Settlement.* Special masters can also be employed as mediators, particularly in difficult-to-settle cases. They can facilitate settlement negotiations and conduct settlement conferences.

Like special masters, court-appointed experts can be helpful in complex matters. The court may call upon an expert, to, among other things, shed light on a selected area of a highly technical or scientific case.

[This section will] explore in greater detail the roles of special masters and court-appointed experts.

DISCOVERY MANAGEMENT

Because exploitation of liberal discovery rules is a major contributor to high costs and delays in litigation, discovery has been the focus of a number of reform efforts. The American Bar Association's Special Committee on Discovery Abuse, for example, addressed the problems of discovery and recommended changes to establish greater judicial control over cases, improve discovery practices, and promote professionalism among lawyers. The recommendations became the basis for many of the 1981 and 1983 revisions to the federal discovery rules. (See, e.g., Federal Rules of Civil Procedure 11, 16, 26 (f) and (g), and 34.) Local federal district courts have also instituted changes to improve the discovery process. For example, the United States District Court for the Eastern District of New York implemented, on an experimental basis, such reforms as telephone conferencing, increased use of magistrates, and greater emphasis on sanctions.

Exploitation of liberal discovery results in poorly planned, unfocused dispute resolution. The proposals presented in this section are designed to make discovery—and hence dispute resolution—more manageable and efficient. (See also Sobel, Proposal for Abbreviating Complex Civil Cases in Early Disposition Strategies section. Sobel makes additional suggestions for controlling discovery.)

PROPOSALS FOR REDUCING DISCOVERY COSTS

This proposal, by Theodore A. Groenke of Chicago's McDermott, Will & Emery is most appropriate for simpler cases, such as repetitive product liability cases brought by individual plaintiffs, but can also be used in more complex matters.

Groenke's proposal builds on the 1983 amendments to Rule 16(b) of the Federal Rules of Civil Procedure. To achieve early identification of both contested and uncontested fact issues, disputing parties would be required to exchange a description of issues and the facts necessary to resolve them within sixty days after the date of a standing order issued promptly after commencement of the action. At this time, the parties would also be required to exchange all documents they plan to use as trial exhibits or in trial preparation, and to provide a list of all witnesses. Within thirty days after exchanging this information, parties would stipulate to material facts that are uncontested, and arrive at a final discovery plan for additional facts. If the parties cannot agree on a discovery plan on their own, the court would impose a mandatory and final discovery plan. The scope of discovery would be governed by a "substantial need" standard, rather than the more liberal Rule 26 test.

NEUTRAL DISCOVERY MANAGERS

Richard M. Rosenbleeth of Philadelphia's Blank, Rome, Cominsky & McCauley believes complex cases cannot be significantly streamlined without firm external control over the process. Although judges have the authority to manage and guide the discovery process, they often lack the time. Rosenbleeth thus proposes creating panels of respected former judges and senior attorneys to supervise discovery in complex litigation.

Compensated at (or close to) their regular hourly rates, panelists would have extensive experience in complex litigation, such as antitrust, securities, construction, product liability, or trademark matters. Among other things, panelists could rule on disputes arising during discovery, ascertain the good faith compliance with discovery orders, make preliminary rulings on privilege claims, and supervise discovery generally. Panelists would be appointed to an individual case pursuant to

Rule 53 of the Federal Rules of Civil Procedure (or similar rules in state courts). Parties would play an important or even determinative role in selecting the panel.

Because panelists would be burdened by fewer institutional restraints than judges or magistrates are, they could meet with counsel in a wider range of settings. For example, they could be present during the taking of a deposition. In addition, if the panelist were an expert in the substance of the dispute, he might be able to anticipate and identify discovery abuses more quickly than a judge or magistrate could. Panelists would also have more time than a court has to devote to the discovery phase of a case. In general, through their flexibility and access to counsel, panelists have the potential to improve the efficiency of the discovery process. (For additional information on special masters as discovery managers, see McGovern, Use of Masters and Magistrates in Complex Litigation, in Section V.)

ADMISSIONS PRACTICE

Proposed by Thomas W. Evans of New York's Mudge Rose Guthrie Alexander & Ferdon, admissions practice is an attempt to break through entrenched practices that too often turn discovery into a wasteful, counterproductive process instead of a useful litigation aid.

Evans defines admissions practice as the successive use of request for admission under Rule 36, together with related enforcement provisions, discovery and pre-trial conferences, to narrow issues and requirements of proof in litigation. Simultaneous service of a single omnibus interrogatory requesting reasons for denial can add to the efficacy of the process.

Although requests for admission have increased five-fold since the significant expansion of Rule 36 in 1970, they still represent a small percentage of discovery mechanisms currently in use, in part because the rules are clouded by a number of misunderstandings. For example, many lawyers use request for admission only in relation to documents, even though the scope is much broader.

The rule also has teeth: Under Rule 37(c), the court can award reasonable expenses, including attorneys' fees to a party that has been put to its proof by an unreasonable failure to admit. Currently, however, this sanction is very rarely used.

Admissions practice has the potential to define issues early in the case, eliminate unnecessary issues, limit the scope of discovery, and reduce the breadth and complexity of matters presented at trial. In short, the technique can make discovery more useful and efficient.

SUMMARY JUDGMENT

This section contains proposals for using summary judgment and partial summary judgment to resolve or narrow critical issues early in the lawsuit, reduce court congestion, save money for parties and courts, promote speedy resolution, or facilitate early settlement.

PROPOSAL FOR INCREASED USE

In his chapter [in the book *ADR and the Courts*] Robert N. Sayler of Washington, D.C.'s Covington & Burling maintains that the promise of Rule 56 is unfulfilled. The problem is not in the rule itself, for it says essentially the right things and establishes the right burdens. Instead, the problem lies in its implementation: inadequate procedures to test the materiality and substantiality of alleged fact disputes, frequent unwillingness of bench and bar to grapple with summary adjudication until the eve of trial, a nonchalance about the utility and importance of the rule, and the growth of a number of doctrines threatening to strangle it.

After examining the reluctance of bench and bar to embrace Rule 56 and reap its benefits, Sayler proposes three strategies for more effective summary judgment practice. First he suggests that parties be required to submit a statement of undisputed material facts with each summary judgment motion.

Second, he recommends a two-step procedure for testing the substantiality and materiality of alleged fact disputes. The initial step is the present Rule 56 procedure supplemented by the statement of undisputed material facts. The second step is a pre-trial conference under Rule 16 during which the judge questions the parties on their evidentiary submissions.

Third, to deter dilatory tactics by parties opposing Rule 56 motions, Sayler suggests greater use of Rule 11 and Rule 56(g) economic sanctions against counsel and client.

Sayler concludes with a variety of suggestions for bench and bar to encourage the rule's application in appropriate instances. For example, he suggests that trial judges become more receptive to summary judgment motions, especially once discovery has been completed. Sayler also recommends that trial lawyers pay more (and earlier) attention to the potential for summary judgment disposition of cases or significant issues. In short, Sayler believes that to secure "just, speedy and inexpensive" dispute resolution—Rule 1's command—Rule 56 must have great prominence.

FACILITATING SETTLEMENT THROUGH PARTIAL SUMMARY JUDGMENT

Jay F. Lapin of Washington, D.C.'s Wilmer, Cutler & Pickering proposes selective use of partial summary judgment to identify and resolve critical legal issues early in the lawsuit. Once key legal issues are resolved, parties can often narrow their remaining differences and settle the entire dispute.

Lapin suggests that instead of depending on litigants to present such issues, judges should take the initiative and explore with parties whether there are issues that are ripe for judicial decision and whose resolution would facilitate settlement. By taking the initiative, the court relieves parties of the difficulty or awkwardness that sometimes accompanies the first move toward settlement.

This approach is well-suited to many types of issues. For example, a dispute over the availability, as a matter of law, of punitive damages may obstruct settlement of a contract action even if parties are otherwise prepared to compromise on liability for other types of compensatory damages. The availability of punitive damages may turn on a legal issue such as choice of law. Resolution of that legal issue through partial summary judgment can enhance the parties' ability to settle the entire lawsuit.

In short, if the court takes a more activist approach to inquiring whether there are motions that will streamline litigation or aid in settlement, the judicious use of partial summary judgment can reduce, not increase, the burden faced by trial courts.

TABLE 1
PRIMARY DISPUTE RESOLUTION PROCESSES[3]

Characteristics	Adjudication	Arbitration[4]	Mediation	Negotiation
Voluntary/ Involuntary	Involuntary	Voluntary	Voluntary	Voluntary
Binding/ Nonbinding	Binding, subject to appeal	Binding, subject to review on limited grounds	If agreement, enforcement as contract	If agreement, enforceable as contract
Third Party	Imposed, third-party neutral decisionmaker, generally with no specialized experience in dispute subject	Party-selected outside facilitator, usually with specialized subject expertise	Party-selected outside facilitator, usually with specialized subject expertise	No third-party facilitator
Degree of Formality	Formalized and highly structured by predetermined, rigid rules	Usually informal, unstructured	Usually informal, unstructured	Usually informal, unstructured
Nature of Proceeding	Opportunity for each party to present proofs and arguments	Unbounded presentation of evidence, arguments and interests	Unbounded presentation of evidence, arguments and interests	Unbounded presentation of evidence, arguments and interests
Outcome	Principled decision, supported by reasoned opinion	Mutually acceptable agreement sought	Mutually acceptable agreement sought	Mutually acceptable agreement sought
Private/Public	Public	Private	Private	Private

---

3 Tables 1 and 2 are reprinted with permission of Stephen B. Goldberg, Eric D. Green and Frank E.A. Sander, *Dispute Resolution*, Little, Brown & Co.

4 Court-annexed arbitration is involuntary, nonbinding and public

TABLE 2

"HYBRID" DISPUTE RESOLUTION PROCESSES

Characteristics	Private Judging	Neutral Expert Fact-Finding	Mini-Trial	Ombudsman	Summary Jury Trial
Voluntary/ Involuntary	Voluntary	Voluntary or involuntary under FRE 706	Voluntary	Voluntary	Involuntary
Binding/ Nonbinding	Binding, subject to appeal	Nonbinding but results may be admissible	If agreement, enforcement as contract	Nonbinding	Nonbinding
Third Party	Party-selected third-party decisionmaker, may have to be former judge or lawyer	Third-party neutral with specialized subject matter expertise; may be selected by the parties or the court	Party-selected neutral advisor, sometimes with specialized subject expertise	Third party selected by institution	Mock jury impaneled by Court
Degree of Formality	Statutory procedure but highly flexible as to timing, place and procedures	Informal	Less formal than adjudication; procedural rules may be set by parties	Informal	Procedural rules fixed; less formal than adjudication
Nature of Proceeding	Opportunity for each party to present proofs and arguments	Investigatory	Opportunity and responsibility to present summary proofs and arguments	Investigatory	Opportunity for each side to present summary proofs and arguments
Outcome	Principled decision, sometimes supported by findings of fact and conclusions of law	Report or testimony	Mutually acceptable agreement sought	Report	Advisory verdict
Private/ Public	Private, unless judicial enforcement sought	Private, unless disclosed in court	Private	Private	Usually public

5 WITHOUT PREJUDICE

*The law, like the traveler, must be ready
for the morrow.*

—Benjamin Cardozo, *The Growth of the Law*

THIS PROPOSED NEW EDUCATIONAL PROGRAM would allow rank-and-file lawyers and ordinary business people to learn about, adopt and adapt ADR into their local communities. It would be an ongoing educational, information exchange that could be a valuable coordinating vehicle for the legal profession.

When one enters into the very exciting area of ADR coordinators or departments in law firms, the fun really begins, and in this regard there are several precedents. A number of firms in Canada are either launching or at least seriously considering ADR coordinators and departments. *Without Prejudice* would provide a way to effectively share the trials and tribulations of these profoundly important issues. One issue becoming more paramount is the economics of justice. A former president of a major American corporation is quoted as saying: "We gave our lawyers an unlimited budget and they still exceeded it!"

Several initiatives could be undertaken to integrate the whole ADR spectrum into the community. In the Regional Municipality of Ottawa-Carleton, we have contacts and resources that we could immediately draw upon to conduct training workshops and present ADR orientation sessions. The Canadian Institute for Conflict Resolution (CICR) could be used as a resource for training. Professor Brian Mandell, at the Norman Paterson School of International Affairs at Carleton University and a Fellow and Director of Research at CICR, will assist in the program and training development. There are many lawyers in Ottawa who can offer ideas and skills, and several business people and many others involved in other disciplines who would participate, either as members or ADR suppliers, and would submit ideas and help in implementation.

It is suggested that we at CICR must soon announce a national, neutral program for lawyers and business people that is supported by the major groups interested in this subject (legal, business, arbitrators, mediators who could also be litigants or other lawyers interested in the firm). If we do not proceed with a program some other body will, or there will be a confusing or inefficient proliferation.

Without Prejudice would provide a vehicle to confer together and would assist law firms in adding ADR services to the firm's services and would also provide assistance to non-lawyers involved in ADR.

THEORY AND STRUCTURE

The following is a preliminary outline of the theory and structure of *Without Prejudice*:

WITHOUT PREJUDICE
A WIN-WIN APPROACH TO A WIN-WIN SOLUTION

Without Prejudice is an educational program designed to promote training, program and resource development, and implementation of the full spectrum of ADR attitudes and processes, from negotiation to litigation, for the corporate and legal sectors.

ADR's continued growth is inevitable in Canada. Research and networking in jurisdictions around the world has led us to believe that it is time to seriously consider introducing a national, neutral, self-financing program initiated in Canada, independent of any formal legal or business organizations. *Without Prejudice* is suggested as an appropriate vehicle for lawyers and business people to deal with ADR. This program would be run on business-like terms but as a corporation-driven foundation whose net profits would be used to educate the general public about ADR and help implement community-based programs in schools and neighbourhood justice centres. A similar program could also be promoted in the U.S., where the trade mark is also registered, and in other jurisdictions.

In order to facilitate *Without Prejudice,* a financial base is required. Therefore, businesses and law firms would be asked to pay annual membership fees. Local volunteer executives would operate the local chapter, which would be led by a locally paid director. Net revenues would be applied to the objectives of the program.

The *Without Prejudice* project is meant to be a part of the ADR reality in Canada for the benefit of lawyers and their clients, and business people and their industries. The following outline is a statement of some of its benefits, principles, and objectives; the actual details and mechanics of the program would be determined in consultation with the legal and business sectors (since it will be their program, in practical terms). The program will evolve and be adapted by members as their operations, aspirations, and needs dictate.

PROGRAM STRUCTURE

▨ The program will be an economical, national, self-financing ADR vehicle for the legal and business community. The program will operate on business-like principles. Public and other private donations will be sought to help meet the objectives for the benefit of the program members. All net profits will be used to meet the objectives of the program or donated to charitable works in the area of ADR.

▨ The program will be organized by provincial sectors, each with its own volunteer executive and a salaried director, if warranted. Each local chapter will receive a licence with simplified terms and conditions so there is integrity in the program objectives and name, but each local chapter will have total flexibility.

▨ Members will include law firms or businesses, and individual lawyers and business people. Other institutions and groups could form divisions of the program.

PROGRAM OBJECTIVES

▨ Reduce stress on courts, judges and lawyers by emphasizing the role of the individual disputant and his/her professional advisors, and by providing lawyers with a menu of alternatives for clients. Business members would sign ADR pledges similar to those signed by 350 *Fortune* companies in the U.S. with the Center for Public Resources

▨ Explore ways to involve ADR in law practices, e.g., through ADR coordinators or departments, and in various industries. These industries could establish their own ADR processes.

▨ Provide a neutral forum for members to learn about and evaluate private ADR suppliers (e.g., arbitrators, mediators, private courts) and share experiences about those suppliers. The program will not provide any direct ADR services, but could create a database of ADR suppliers and invite the suppliers to make their services known to program members.

▨ Provide an efficient method to study and implement ADR processes without every jurisdiction having to reinvent the wheel.

▨ Develop a workable partnership for the legal and business professions with those involved in the administration of justice.

▨ Develop effective communications and draw upon resources with other groups with extensive ADR experience, e.g., in the U.S., the Center for Public Resources (CPR), Endispute Inc., the National Conference on Peace and Conflict Resolution (NCPCR), Society for Professionals in Dispute Resolution (SPIDR), and the National Institute for Dispute Resolution (NIDR); in Australia, the Conflict Resolution Network; and in Canada, the Justice Institute of British Columbia and the Network for Community

Justice and Conflict Resolution in Kitchener, Ontario. The program will also draw extensively on family and labour practitioners, law precedents and experiences, and other groups and cultures with ADR components.

- Create and maintain an independent program that is also tied into the good of the community as a whole, which will also serve to enhance the image and create a better understanding of the bar.

PROGRAM BENEFITS

Member firms and their employees would receive:

- Reduced-price courses on conflict resolution and management skills. Reduced-price brochures, readable papers and workshops will also be developed for employees to help reduce stress and conflict in the workplace
- Initial documentation on dispute resolution
- Newsletters on various alternative dispute resolution mechanisms, including arbitration, mediation, conciliation, mini-trials, summary-jury trial, case evaluation, fact finding, and expert assistance
- Opportunities to network with other members with similar interests in the business and legal communities
- Affiliations with scholars on a national interdisciplinary basis and access to the latest research on ADR.

6 CONFERENCES

*Expedience and justice frequently are
not even on speaking terms.*
—Michigan Senator Arthur H. Vandenberg

IN THIS CHAPTER I briefly describe some of the conferences that either I or others attended, and highlight conferences coming up in the next year.

1988 CONFERENCES

American Bar Association
MEDIATION AND EDUCATION
April 8–10, 1988
Washington, D.C.

The book of materials at this conference noted that on August 2, 1986, the ABA Standing Committee on Dispute Resolution was charged by its House of Delegates to:

> "study, experiment with, disseminate information concerning, and support with appropriate institutionalization of methods for the resolution of disputes other than the traditional litigation processes, including six major objectives; clearinghouse and technical assistance to other ABA Divisions and the 350 dispute resolutions nationwide; active lawyers' involvement with these associations; conduct educational programs; develop alternative career opportunities for lawyers; conduct research for programs and legislative models; develop innovative programs, e.g., Multi-Door Dispute Resolution Project."

About 400 people attended, and approximately 60 cooperating agencies were represented at this conference, which was co-sponsored by the U.S. White House Office of Consumer Affairs, the National Association of Mediation in Education, Federation of Teachers (600,000 strong) and the International Creativity Office, which was established by world-renowned educator and creativity expert, Dr. Edward De Bono. In his remarks, Dr. De Bono reminded us that with ADR we should avoid the Western approach (i.e., abolish the existing system and start something hitherto untried, then be left in chaos) and instead adopt an Oriental approach (maintain and improve the existing system and also provide appropriate and better alternatives). The who's who of educational bodies was represented as were other prestigious groups, including the American Arbitrators' Association, and a number of law scholars and ADR leaders, including Frank Sander of the Harvard Law School.

The President of the ABA, Robert MacCrate, put the conference in the context of a wise and long view of world peace and the next generation, stressing the role of lawyers in engaging in the art of problem-solving at all levels of society. Conference organizer Prue Kestner, Assistant Staff Director of the ADR Committee, who has been most helpful to us, also spoke about the relevance of the school programs to our general social understanding.

A 425-page book of precedents was distributed, with information on school peer mediation programs, conflict skills curriculums, and other general literature about ADR.

Woodroffe High School Principal Christine Hubbard, Vice-Principal Ivan Roy, Project Coordinator Cheryl Picard and I made a presentation at a workshop about the Woodroffe High School pilot project, which is not only the first project of its type in Canada but also the most recent in North America (see Chapter 9 for more on the Woodroffe High School pilot project). Other workshop presenters were educators from Hawaii (including Professor Mel Ezer), who were acknowledged to have initiated the concept of mediation in education about seven years ago. The conference left an indelible impact on our awareness of the meaning of these endeavours for our times and future generations.

CONFERENCE ON ACCESS TO JUSTICE
Ministry of the Attorney General of Ontario
June 20–22, 1988
Toronto, Ontario

This conference, attended by approximately 325 people from Canada and abroad, was hailed by some scholars as the most comprehensive review in Canada of justice in the late twentieth century. In his program comments, the Honourable Ian Scott wrote:

> To my knowledge this is the first time politicians, lawyers, judges, interest groups and other concerned individuals have met together to consider the critical issues we will address over the next few days.

The CICR was privileged to be invited and I enjoyed being a panellist in a workshop on neighbourhood and lay justice. The first two days included plenary sessions, panel discussions, and nine concurrent workshops.

On the last day, four speakers gave their views on "The Challenge Ahead: From Ideas to Action." Senator Jean Bazin acknowledged that access to justice was one of the most serious social problems in Canada. He urged national debate and encouraged participants to discern hard facts and real solutions and their costs. June Callwood, a governor of the CICR, emphasized that Canada cannot succeed as a nation unless we can succeed in the neighbourhood, and she stressed the importance of children. She recommended that when the court becomes the high-tech last resort, responsibility must go back to the family and the community. She acknowledged how educational, health and legal institutions meet certain social needs, but added that we need "frontline skills on a human scale." She stated that the conference was a magnificent first step for humankind and the world village.

Harvey J. Bliss, then president of the CBA-Ontario, delivered a paper entitled *A Lawyer's View of Access to Justice,* the executive summary of which is below:

> Harvey Bliss begins by reminding us of the necessity to maintain a good justice system, regardless of the cost. Indeed he contends that gross under-funding and public apathy are the twin threats to the legal system. The present system is structurally sound and, although there is a continuing duty to seek better and cheaper methods, will work effectively if properly funded. To reinforce his point, he explains different facets of the justice system—legal aid, legal insurance, court jurisdiction, alternative dispute resolution, paralegals, contingency fees, and the like—and suggests how they can be used and improved to make the legal process more accessible and just.
>
> A significant part of the paper deals with the empirical study, as described by Bogart and Vidmar, which was commissioned for this conference. He is of the view that "full confidence cannot be placed in the results" and he charts some of the technical difficulties he perceives with its design and implementation. Nevertheless, he does think that the results are by and large encouraging. Finally, he urges lawyers and the public to work together to make the present system the best and most efficient it can be.

The Attorney General is seeking follow-up input from participants and, given the growing awareness and development of ADR and its profound evolving relationship to the social order, the creation of an advisory committee may be of use to the government, the legal profession and the public.

American Bar Association
110TH ANNUAL MEETING
August 4–11, 1988
Toronto, Ontario

This mammoth conference drew more than 20,000 people and $25 million to Toronto, and resulted in a further healthy cooperation between CBA and ABA. It included a number of sessions involving ADR.

I attended only the workshop called "ADR—Is it for Real" organized by the Tort and Insurance Practice Section. Four papers were delivered. Professor Nancy Rogers presented an overview of ADR, a review of the last decade and a short preview of the next.

George A. McKeon, General Counsel of The Travelers Companies, explained that ADR was unknown to the company before 1983 when an ADR program began in its claims department, but became an integral part of its litigation management program in 1985. In 1987, almost 3,000 of 5,500 court cases were settled by ADR. In 1986 a project known as The Connecticut ADR Project Inc., involving 27 insurance companies, further successfully promoted ADR. (See Chapter 8 for more information about The Connecticut ADR Project.) Mr. McKeon stated that although many plaintiffs were initially reluctant to hire ADR suppliers to help resolve cases, this attitude is changing. A private company in Canada has already begun to deal with insurance companies in ADR processes. He also mentioned that the private bar will be required by in-house counsel to learn about the use of ADR. As a further example, he referred to the Cleveland Project, which involves more than 25 trial specialists of the Cleveland Bar whose objective is "to move ADR into the mainstream of legal practice, and to promote its use in the business, legal and insurance communities." He ended with this admonition to the private bar: "What you have to gain is much greater than what you have to lose."

A thoughtful and articulate paper was included from Philadelphia lawyer Arthur G. Raynes, entitled, "Weathering the Storm: A trial lawyer's response to filial rebellion and ADR." The title refers to his son's refusal to become a lawyer because a law career is "too confining, too tradition-bound and unimaginative" while "getting to the courtroom sometimes takes years, years often filled with tedious discovery and procedural manoeuvring." In his paper he pleaded the case for litigation and identified the legitimate concerns of trial lawyers about the ADR movement. (See Chapter 2 for more detail on trial lawyers' concerns about ADR.) I should note that Mr. Raynes was unable to make the conference, and in his stead he sent an associate who stated to the 75 lawyers, judges and ADR suppliers in the audience that the litigation bar is fed up with those people in ADR who treat them like the evil empire, and that some ADR approaches are not enamouring trial lawyers to the "movement." This momentary airing of dirty laundry was most interesting for me because it provided further incentive to propose that a different philosophical approach may be needed for ADR to overcome this ironic conflict between some of those in ADR and in the litigation bar. (See Chapter 3 for details on the proposed new philosophical approach.)

The fourth paper was by Judge Frank G. Evans, Chief Justice of the First Judicial District Court of Appeals in Houston, Texas, who had chaired the

ABA-Mediation in Education Conference in Washington in April 1988. Judge Evans showed a creative new video that included such clips as "The Case of the Rotten Apples" and "In Search of Mega Moola" that depicted five different processes to settle a dispute: moderated settlement, mediation, arbitration, summary jury trial, and mini-trial. He noted that a principal difficulty with ADR is that few people really understand the terminology. Alternative dispute resolution and its acronym ADR are still new concepts to most people, and the terms mediation and mini-trials are even less understood. Because arbitration is so well known, many people consider ADR an arbitrated process. (Interestingly, in our community initiatives we have encountered this very problem in seeking to implement ADR processes.) He concluded as follows: "The cooperative effort of lawyers and judges in the appropriate use of ADR will assure greater citizen access to justice and will also permit judges and court staff to focus attention on those cases that do require formal court adjudication."

Association Internationale des Jeunes Avocats (AIJA) –
International Association of Young Lawyers

XXVI CONGRESS
September 5–9, 1988
Munich, Germany

This international conference attracted me for only one reason—the session by the International Arbitration Commission on Alternative Methods of Dispute Resolution. About 600 lawyers from 35 countries attended, including approximately 20 lawyers from both Canada and the United States. The ADR seminar was the best attended. Thirteen nations reported on ADR activities in their countries: Brazil, Canada, Denmark, England and Wales, Finland, France, the Far East (particularly China), India, Ireland, the Netherlands, Spain, Sweden, and the United States. The moderator was Dr. Glossner from France, Chairman of the ADR Committee for the AIJA; he delivered a memorable concluding address encouraging settlement with the motto that "the best arbitration is no arbitration at all," and encouraged lawyers to be problem solvers with the objective of "dispute containment." Another paper included a treatise on technical expertise—a supplemental means to prevent or settle commercial disputes.

The papers of these 13 participating nations are summarized below:

BRAZIL

The presenter referred to "the delay and bureaucracy of the Brazilian judiciary" resulting in either arbitration or out-of-court settlements to "avoid high costs (and) loss of time and the need to contract expert proof, which may often be misunderstood by the judge." A rule of court in Brazil defines doctrine of settlement in the prejudicial and litigation phase: "It is lawful for the interested parties to prevent or end the litigation by means of mutual concessions." The settlement reached is considered *res judicata* except in the case of "malice, violence, or essential error as to the disputed thing." Problems concerning the arbitration alternative involve delay. A new arbitration law is awaited. The presenter repeated a sentiment well known to trial lawyers since time immemorial, that "in other cases, (the parties) may not be interested in a quick solution and even may resort to bad faith. Litigation and court action is the only solution in these cases."

CANADA (IN FRENCH)

The presenter described mediation as being mostly associated with family law and conciliation with labour law. He added that although these processes are not as well used as they should be, they are gaining attention nationally and internationally, especially with arbitration centres in British Columbia and Quebec. The presenter claimed that Canadian lawyers play a more active role than their European counterparts in acting as third party neutrals. Conciliation and mediation are not clearly defined and are sometimes confused in family law or other general areas. However, they are seen as distinct concepts in labour relations. Federal statutes and provincial statutes in Ontario and Quebec were cited as examples of legislative recognition of mediation in family and labour law.

The presenter also referred to the criminal justice system and pending legislation concerning restitution hearings between victims and offenders.

Pretrials (or prehearings) are described as popular and are becoming more successful as their setups improve. The presenter encouraged the use of quantum-only preparatory conferences so that if liability is established at trial the damages have already been settled.

The presenter complained that Canada has not played the role that it should on the world scene in ADR. He indicated that mini-trials were still unknown in Canada, but predicted that once they are understood their use will spread quickly. The presenter said he looked forward to a promising future with more out-of-court settlements and quicker, cheaper, more efficient and more humane alternatives.

DENMARK

The courts are admonished by the *Administration of Justice Act* to promote an amicable settlement in all civil cases of first instance. Mediation and pre-trials are used. Concern was expressed that some judges do successfully coerce settlements for three key reasons—because they want to avoid writing a judgement or avoid a trial, because of undue influence by a judge who hasn't heard the whole case, and because judges coerce inexperienced lawyers. The professions use mediation extensively to settle internal disputes with parties assisted by counsel.

International arbitration is common because of trade. A small claims court without lawyers is being considered.

ENGLAND AND WALES

Litigation was hailed as a "logical starting point" with the benefits of specialist tribunals within the court system and court use of experts.

Consumer problems are being resolved "quicker, cheaper (with) less formal methods (by) ordinary people without lawyers" by a consumer council. There are also trade association conciliation and arbitration schemes, which are two-tiered processes. However, these schemes are neither well known nor well used by the public. The use of ombudsmen was discussed, especially in insurance banking.

FAR EAST—CHINA

The presenter writes: "According to the Chinese way of thinking and according to Chinese tradition, law has always played, and still plays, a secondary role only." The social order does not deal with personal rights, but duties to neighbours and the community. A court case is a "scandal...troubling the natural and...social order." Settlement is a community virtue and a person who takes another to court, as one author said, is "regarded as disruptive, boorish, and an uncultivated individual who lacks the cardinal virtues of modesty and readiness to compromise." Although there are more laws and Chinese modernization involves building a legal system (largely for international trade), conciliation is still considered the most appropriate way to settle—voluntarily, individually, or through a court committee. Conciliation seems interchangeable with mediation and is considered part of an arbitrator's primary role, again to enhance friendship and trade relations.

The same holds true with Japan and Korea.

FINLAND

The concept of a mini-trial is not known. No formal processes are in place but conciliation and mediation are practiced de facto and are considered interchangeable. Contracts sometimes include these or "negotiate in good faith" clauses with pre-dispute mechanisms that are recognized by the courts. Some are very detailed, but the court will assume jurisdiction if settlement is not achieved. Business people admire settlement; opinions of experts can be obtained, and a law professor's opinion is highly valued. The "new wave" of "dispute resolution settlement procedures has not yet reached (Finnish) shores as a national phenomenon."

FRANCE (IN FRENCH)

The presenter mentioned new rules of conciliation adopted by the International Chamber of Commerce as of January 1, 1988. The theme of conciliation dominates this paper, starting with arbitration as the best-known form of ADR, which evolved out of a historical need for a more efficient, less costly, more harmonious process to help business people resolve their disputes, especially internationally. Describing it as a "rich and subtle" substitute to litigation, the presenter commended it as a "tool of quality" if used "with competence and precaution." French law recognizes the use of a referee before arbitration, but this is seen as a "menace" to arbitration.

The papers mentioned the concept of a "transaction" in which the parties can voluntarily and deliberately abandon certain procedural rights and be bound by the strict wording of the contract, which provides specific consequences for the parties' conduct.

A most interesting concept is the "amiable composition" in which the parties agree to essentially allow intangibles to prevail over specifics, equity over law, goodwill over legal benefits. The third party called upon to intervene and settle the dispute is to be mindful of the "internal public order" and the "national public order" where the domestic law is identified and the legal rights and responsibilities are preserved. The third party is seen as a "moderator," whose mandate is to sense the subjective principles of the disputants' relationship from general statements in the agreement and the parties' situation, and to render an amiable compromise that the parties will honour. Some practitioners are reticent and one lawyer has complained that "disguised in the law an amiable composer seeks to confuse." The spirit of this conciliation approach is also captured in the embodiment in the civil code that allows arbitrators to divulge impressions to the parties before rendering a decision. This affords the parties an opportunity to settle. (This is similar to the mediation-arbitration hybrid being used in some jurisdictions in the United States.) A certain moral authority appears to allow a third-party neutral to function with the respect of the parties as a desirable alternative if the direct, well thought out negotiations fail. The presenter stated that internationally the ideas of conciliation and mediation are more clearly distinguished than in France where there i s a provision for elective conciliation during arbitration. However, the "without prejudice" nature of a conciliation, which could avoid delays, costs, and embroiling business people into an adversarial environment, is attracting more practitioners.

Another type of compromise arrangement involves a more informed observer or third-party neutral advisor who gives an opinion that has no force or effect, and helps point the way to advancing negotiations.

Mini-trials, which are only at the experimental stage in France, are recognized as having grown from the evolution of ADR as a response to the adversarial deficiencies. The presenter predicted that this concept has a "great future in our economic and judicial universe." (At the AIJA conference, Dr. Glossner, the chair of the ADR committee of the AIJA, stated that after reviewing the video on mini-trials, the French bar in Paris reacted by saying it was an "*affronte*.")

In conclusion, the presenter admitted that the presentation was at best only a "rapid tour of the horizon of French ADR methods" and could only hope to "modestly enlighten" the practitioners to explore alternatives to find the most favourable "all to a good end." Given the demands of the international business community for common sense alternatives, the presenter stated that if each alternative keeps its own richness and its appropriateness is determined, the world movement towards ADR is a "justified theme."

INDIA

Arbitration, voluntary or mandatory, is the most popular alternative in the world's most populous democracy, where more than 80 per cent of the population is said to live in rural areas, a substantial percentage of it in poverty.

The parties may, by agreement, state a case before the court. Tribunals deal with employee grievances and other matters, such as tax and customs.

A recent and profound development in India was the landmark judgement delivered in 1986 by the former Chief Justice of the Supreme Court of India, Bragwati C.J. in the case of *Centre for Legal Research and ANR* v. *State of Kerala*, wherein, *inter alia*, the Chief Justice wrote:

> It is absolutely essential that people should be involved in the...program because legal aid is not charity or bounty but it is a social entitlement of people and those in need of legal assistance cannot be looked upon as mere beneficiaries of the legal aid programme but they should be regarded as participants in it.

The judge reviewed the preamble of the 1948 Constitution of India which guarantees citizens "justice" and "equality." The Chief Justice noted that a 1976 amendment required the state to ensure "that the operation of the legal system promotes justice, on a basis of equal opportunity, and shall, in particular, provide free legal aid by suitable legislation or schemes or in any other way to ensure that opportunities for securing justice are not denied to any citizen by reason of economic or other disabilities." He directed the state to create a new order allowing the "grass-roots level" to operate a program known as LOK ADALAT which means "*a provision of justice at the door of a common man,*" based "on the principles of honesty and good conscience" with "its foundation...embodied in Indian culture and civilization" to deal with "the unmet legal needs of the people." By allowing voluntary organizations and social action groups to be directly involved, the court felt that "they have their finger on the pulse of the people...and what measures are necessary to be taken for the purpose of ending…exploitation and injustice and reaching social or distributive justice to (the people)."

Although this judgement is particularly relevant to Indian jurisprudence, it contains universal principles that form the hallmark of our times.

IRELAND

Most cases are settled by court or arbitration. Mediation and conciliation are mostly confined to matrimonial and trade disputes. Experts are used in building contracts or rent renewals because the experts are not arbitrators and can use their own knowledge without reference to the parties. Mini-trials are not practised. Ombudsmen have investigatory functions only.

SPAIN

ADR is acutely needed in Spain, where an expression roughly translates to "Go to court and the devil may take care of the outcome." Court rules were changed in 1984—the first revision since 1881—to encourage reduction of needless litigation. However, the speaker indicated that "litigation still is in Spain a hard and frequently hopeless task."

Arbitration is one main alternative, and new laws for domestic and international matters are encouraging.

A new rule was meant to encourage settlement by conciliation, but in practice does not do so: "After all parties have attended the hearing, the Judge will open the meeting and first of all will exhort them to settle. If the outcome is positive it will be recorded in the minutes which will be signed by the Judge…" However, conciliation is successful in labour matters. Conciliation committees have recently been established in the insurance industry. In 1984, a new provision, which is not yet law, provides for ADR in consumer disputes. Rural leases by law embody a conciliation alternative. Expert opinions are used.

SWEDEN

The court is obliged to promote early settlement and, although judges are not supposed to impose settlements, many judges do. The court can call parties to a preliminary hearing for this purpose. The court can appoint a mediator, which is often done in construction disputes. In landlord and tenant disputes, the law requires prior reference to conciliation by a council.

Because of court congestion, mediation is being used much more. Often, retired judges act as mediators in commercial disputes. Mediation is also used in family and labour matters. Mini-trials are not in use.

SWITZERLAND (IN FRENCH)

Two papers were presented by the Swiss delegation. The first one covered conciliation, mediation, arbitration, and expert assistance. In Switzerland, ADR is a healthy development; the presenter favoured the voluntary nature of conciliation and expert arbitrators.

The other presenter concentrated on mini-trials, which are slowly gaining in popularity. He started by criticizing the term "mini-trial," noting that the procedures were simply another form of mediation or conciliation. The Zurich Chamber of Commerce's experience since October 1984 was contrasted with the American style of mini-trials. Four distinct features of the Zurich model set it apart from the American version. First, in Zurich, the panel is composed of three parties: one nominated by each of the parties and a third party mutually selected as the president. Second, the panel makes a unanimous recommendation if the parties do not reach an accord. Third, if a unanimous recommendation is not possible, the president submits a recommendation. Finally, the panel remains present during the negotiations. However, the same reasons compel the continued use of mini-trials in both countries, i.e., the desire for faster, cheaper, less destructive and more private dispute resolution procedures.

Although conciliation is also used, mini-trials are perceived as being "conciliation improved."

Arbitration or litigation is suspended by agreement while dispute resolution is attempted by these other methods.

On a further international note, the Swiss parliament adopted a new law on international arbitration (hailed by one observer as "a significant step towards liberalism") on December 18, 1987, which is anticipated to come into force on January 1, 1989.

As a further example of the wonderful differences of opinion at work, Switzerland pursued an independent solution with its law and rejected the United Nations Commission on Trade Law (UNCITRAL) Model Law as an over-complicated, over-compromised "ready-made, all-year-round suit," despite its adoption by several nations, including Canada, Germany, England and Hong Kong.

UNITED STATES

This conference included a paper delivered by Gabe Shawn Varges of the New York State Bar. His paper is discussed extensively in Chapter 1 in the section entitled "A Lawyer's Account" and his dispute resolution paradigm is included in Appendix A.

Another presenter from the United States, Mr. Jay I. Bomze, a lawyer from Philadelphia, filed a paper concentrating on court-supervised ADR which "seems to be a contradiction of terms; for what is ADR an alternative to, if not the courts? The term ADR has come to embrace all creative methods of increasing the efficiency and effectiveness of dispute resolution, whether in court or out of court." Notwithstanding certain constraints inherent in court-supervised rather than private ADR, "there is a wide range of techniques

which may be utilized to promote the 'just, speedy, and inexpensive determination of every action' (Fed. R. Civ. P.l)".

The presenter provided a representative sampling, since it was not possible to outline "an exhaustive listing of every management technique that has
been implemented in courts across the nation." He described a number of
processes triggered by federal rules, including pre-trial conference, use of magistrates, special masters); summary jury trial and mini-trial) and diversion strategies:
court-annexed arbitration (e.g., Philadelphia's court-administered arbitration;
California's judicial arbitration program; Federal Court's annexed arbitration;
Wayne County (Detroit, Michigan) case evaluation conference); court discretion (e.g., Connecticut fact finders and arbitrators; mediation program of
Eastern District of Michigan); medical malpractice screening panels; and litigant discretion (California's "rent-a-judge"). He succinctly concludes: "Effective
implementation of these methods will leave the adjudication process available
for the quality processing of high-impact cases and provide resolution by means
other than full trial, without compromising an individual's rights and dignity."

TECHNICAL EXPERTISE

A lengthy paper extolled the virtues of arbitration and use of an expert as arbitrator, witness, or advisor in international disputes.

UNITED NATIONS
CONFLICT RESOLUTION CONFERENCE
September 14–16, 1988
New York, New York

An extraordinary gathering took place in New York at the annual conference
of Non-Government Organizations (NGOs) with the theme "The role of the
United Nations in Conflict Resolution, Peace Keeping, and Global Security."
More than 800 NGOs from 42 nations participated. The conference was
opened by Therese P. Sevigny, Under-Secretary General for Public Information,
the highest ranking Canadian serving in the U.N. Secretariat. The Secretary
General, Perez de Cuellar, delivered the keynote address. The two themes
were the growing awareness of the multifariousness of conflict resolution and
the need to develop alternative forms of dispute resolution. A reporter who
attended told us that by the end of the week there was a strong sense of the
reality of the "burgeoning international" social phenomenon of ADR. This
was consistent with every other level of activity that we had experienced. It
was interesting to hear that at another recent meeting, an audience member
asked whether the U.N. could do anything to encourage the widespread use
of ADR. In response the Director of Peace Studies, Robin Ludwig, answered
that such initiatives must come from the outside and referred to the joint

effort by Canadians and Australians to promote an International Year of Conflict Resolution.

Canadian Bar Association, Ontario—Continuing Legal Education
ALTERNATIVE DISPUTE RESOLUTION:
WHAT'S ALL THE FUSS ABOUT AND WHERE IS IT GOING?
October 3, 1988
Toronto, Ontario

This seminar was the front page story in the *Lawyer's Weekly*, Vol. 8 No. 23, Friday, October 21, 1988, and appeared under the headline "Alternative Dispute Resolution—Either get on board—or get out of the way?"

The keynote panellist was the Hon. Ian Scott, who remarked that the bad news was how little the Ontario Bar liked ADR, and pointed to the low attendance of about 50 people. The good news, according to Mr. Scott, was how admirably an acorn can grow.

Mr. Scott stressed how lawyers have to break away from the court-dominated culture of training and ethos, and participate in non-adversarial processes as problem solvers. He cited statistics that show trials are the tip of the iceberg in dispute resolution. Lawyers are being consulted in only 30 per cent of civil dispute matters and of those, between 90 and 95 per cent are settled before trial.

Professor Paul Emond from Osgoode Law School delivered a conceptual overview and announced that a major Toronto law firm would soon be announcing a joint ADR program with an accounting firm. He suggested a continuum of dispute resolution models and explained his thesis: "that the ADR movement challenges traditional modes of dispute resolution and invites disputants to search for new and more effective ways of resolving disputes." He spoke of "dispute managers" analyzing which dispute best fits which process. Professor Emond wondered why ADR is not used if it is becoming so popular. I suggested that one solution was a real hands-on locally based educational program through which rank-and-file lawyers and business people could learn about ADR and implement it by using existing professionals and creating new processes in their communities. (See Chapter 5 for more information on the proposed educational program, *Without Prejudice*.) He also stated, and I agree, that ADR is not a panacea and is not meant to replace traditional forms of dispute resolution. It is meant to supplement and not supplant the traditional court process.

He concluded by noting a positive aspect of the ADR movement: "to bring into focus the alternative processes and suggest an approach [in which] the process better fit[s] the problem and the desired result."

John Kelly, the chair of the ADR Committee for the Ontario section of the CBA, made a very interesting presentation. He stated that ADR is in its "infancy" and unless lawyers become knowledgeable and involved and take the lead, they will be led. Responding to the Attorney General's earlier statement that sometimes one has to "bend the arm of the bar," to bring about legislated changes, Mr. Kelly strongly urged his colleagues to consider this as a new business challenge, to "lose fear of the unknown by learning about ADR, and lose fear of lost income by realizing the financial rewards of becoming involved and the financial pitfalls of being extremely short-sighted." He talked about training programs and—after touching upon negotiation, mediation, arbitration, private adjudication, and hybrids thereof—invited the bar to meet "the exciting challenges available to us in a rewarding and constantly evolving field." Mr. Kelly added that the members of the bar should be in the "forefront" rather than having the attitude of "take shelter and hope it all goes away." Mr. Kelly cited the following statistics:

By 1986 there were more than 350 mediation programs in operation in the United States. There are in excess of 20,000 community mediators practising today. More than 20 states have specific dispute resolution statutes and over 120 state bar associations have established committees on dispute resolution. In addition, by 1986, 18 states and federal district courts had instituted mandatory court-annexed arbitration programs; 20 state legislatures have enacted laws requiring the promotion or funding of dispute resolution procedures; 16 federal judges and over 100 state judges have integrated dispute resolution techniques into their courtroom procedures; 260 of the *Fortune* 500 corporate counsel have utilized or otherwise pledged their support for dispute resolution procedures; approximately 108 law schools now offer courses, clinics or other programs in dispute resolution; 1,000 attorneys offer mediation services on child custody and visitation disputes; at least 10 of the major law firms in the United States have established dispute resolution departments or designated dispute resolution partners and associates. The scope of this paper does not allow for an in depth analysis of the plethora of programs offered at the community, state and federal levels in the United States. That has been done admirably by Pat Pitsula in her report on Alternative Dispute Resolution Projects in April of 1987 and Andrew J. Pirie in his consultation paper for the Law Reform Commission in April of 1987 dealing with the present state and future direction of dispute resolution in Canada. Of particular interest however, to lawyers, is the Program On Negotiation at Harvard Law School. This is an applied research centre committed to improving the theory and practice of negotiation in dispute resolution. The program combines the skills of students and staff from different disciplines and professions in the Boston area. Courses in negotiation and mediation are offered to undergraduates, practising lawyers and others involved in the field at Harvard University and M.I.T. as well as many other universities, and provide excellent foundations in the basic skills relating to dispute resolution.

THE RESULT?

Notwithstanding the statistics cited there is a substantial division of opinion over whether these alternative dispute resolution techniques are recognized and used. Corporations regularly use some techniques such as the mini-trial, arbitration, and the summary jury trial, and the criminal diversion programs in the neighbourhood justice centres appear to meet some needs of the community. However, the vast majority of Americans (both lawyers and citizens) appear to know very little about ADR. Although there are many reasons for the apparent lack of public recognition and use—a lack of information and publicity, and a mistrust of new concepts are but two reasons—it seems clear that one of the main causes of the relatively slow growth is the reluctance of lawyers to become involved in the process and to recommend it to their clients. Studies suggest that potential users are clients who rely upon the advice of their solicitors. If the solicitors do not recommend the process, the client will not use it.

There are numerous reasons for the failure of solicitors to recommend the processes, including:

1. lack of knowledge of the existence of these programs;
2. lack of understanding of how the programs work;
3. fear of an unknown process and unwillingness to change the structured methods of resolving disputes through the adjudication process;
4. fear that involvement in ADR will substantially reduce income; and
5. fear that involvement in the process will remove a portion of an existing client base.

Christine Medzcky presented an overview of ADR processes, including those mentioned by Mr. Kelly and others, including neutral-expert fact-finding, mini-trial, summary jury trial, and moderated settlement conference. The Honourable Madam Commissioner Gertrude Speigel spoke extensively on the expanding use of arbitration and used yet another expression to describe ADR: Better Dispute Resolution (BDR). She believes that the recently announced private court in Toronto (like "rent-a-judge" in California) is not distinguishable from arbitration except that its procedures are more closely modelled after public courts. I have heard that some officials criticize the appropriation of the word court.

Robert Blair of Stockwood, Blair, Spies, and Ashby, began by stating that "despite all recent fanfare, the concept of resolving private disputes by methods outside of the public court system is not novel." He stated that there was a "new and reviewed impetus" to develop "extra-judicial" methods due to litigation burden, costs, speed, the need for more flexibility, certainty, and the need to avoid wasting resources. He suggested that we avoid the "war mentality."

He also referred to CPR's program, in which more than half the *Fortune* 500 companies have signed the ADR pledge. (See Chapter 5 for more details on the CPR program.)

1989 CONFERENCES

Most of the time we don't communicate, we just take turns talking.
—Dr. Robert Anthony, *Think*

Although future reading of this book will render the following short list of upcoming conferences seemingly obsolete, this list also serves to provide more examples of the type of activity taking place in ADR, which will likely increase in the years to come.

THE NATIONAL CONFERENCE ON PEACEMAKING AND CONFLICT RESOLUTION (NCPCR)
February 28–March 5, 1989
Montreal, Quebec

The conference will feature an extensive review of ADR with more than 160 workshops, seminars, panels, and training in all aspects of conflict resolution. It is expected that up to 1,500 people will participate. We established good contact with officials of NCPCR when we attended the ABA Workshop Conference on Mediation in Education. Its director at that time, Joel Stronberg, attended our Conflict Resolution Day of Ottawa-Carleton, "Justice is…Just Us" Conference on September 29, 1988. This NCPCR Conference should prove valuable.

American Bar Association
111TH ANNIVERSARY MEETING
August 3–10, 1989
Honolulu, Hawaii

It is most important and very significant to note that, as far as I have been able to ascertain, for the first time in its history the ABA is dedicating its entire annual conference this year to one theme—namely, ADR. The conference is entitled "Resolving Disputes in Pacific Ways." We hope to be involved in the conference in some way. The title not only reflects the area of experience that ADR will be drawn from, but also seems to encourage people to begin to think in ways that are different from their own cultural perspectives.

1988 CONFERENCES IN OTHER DISCIPLINES

I believe that ADR will begin to appear on many more conference agendas dealing with the entire range of legal subjects. Here are some conferences in other disciplines that include segments on ADR:

THE CANADIAN INSTITUTE CONFERENCE
ON COMPUTERS
September 27, 1988

At this conference there was a 45-minute section on "Alternative Dispute Resolution in the High Tech Area."

THIRD ANNUAL CANADIAN CONFERENCE
ON FAMILY MEDIATION
October 22–25, 1988
Quebec City

This conference, which had the theme "Breaking Barriers," included workshops and seminars concerning mediation beyond family law.

Institute for International Research
ALTERNATIVE DISPUTE RESOLUTION—THE LATEST IN CORPORATE
APPLICATIONS AND LEGAL IMPLICATIONS
March 8–9, 1989
Toronto, Ontario

This group has organized a workshop called "Alternative Dispute Resolution—The Latest in Corporate Applications and Legal Implications." It looks well set up. One of the key organizers is Jack Miller, a senior lawyer with one of Canada's largest law firms, Fasken Martineau Walker. Mr. Miller has been a dedicated, long-time proponent of ADR. (This is the type of ongoing workshop that lawyers and business people would conduct themselves under the proposed *Without Prejudice* program. See Chapter 5.) Except for a guest from Connecticut, all presenters will be lawyers from Toronto and Montreal, and other people associated with Canadian organizations familiar with this topic.

As with learning how to cook, we need to get in the kitchen—not just keep studying the cookbook. Thus, we need to have such meetings but we also need to put them into local practice. It is not economical for everyone to fly to a conference to attend seminars but then not have a way to share their ADR experiences, so local adoption will be critical. The local chapters of *Without Prejudice* could remove these inhibitions to ADR development.

7 ADR ORGANIZATIONS

What we call results are beginnings.
—Ralph Waldo Emerson, *Conduct of Life*

NUMEROUS ADR ORGANIZATIONS already exist, and many others are about to begin operations. According to one report, more than 50 U.S. organizations provide ADR services. For example, a Seattle lawyer has established a United States Arbitration and Mediation franchise, while a Philadelphia-based company, Judicate Inc., employs nearly 500 retired judges in a national private court system. In fact, some claim that Judicate is becoming so lucrative that it is drawing away potential judges and encouraging early retirement from the court. The company recently offered its shares to the public and raised millions of dollars.

Bob Raven, President of the ABA, who favours alternatives as adjuncts to the court, is concerned that less attention is being paid to needed reforms in the legal system. More bar associations are active in setting up ADR panels, with some arguing that the profession will fully awaken only with leadership from the top. Law firms that don't embrace ADR will fail to meet clients' demands for alternatives. But, like anything else, new challenges are sure to arise, such as third party malpractice liability, competence issues with mediators and arbitrators, questions of learning, accreditation, threats to precedent, economic abuse, and issues with ethics, public accountability, trust, integrity, credibility, and a new type of elitism.

As an indication of the growing acceptance of ADR, in this chapter I identify a handful of the established ADR organizations.

UNITED STATES

Four organizations are:

1. AMERICAN INTERMEDIATION SERVICE (AIS)

In a letter received October 4, 1988 from the managing mediator, whom I met at the ABA Conference in Toronto, AIS was described as follows:

As we discussed, AIS is an independent dispute resolution firm with its head-quarters in San Francisco and with satellite offices around the country. We have mediated cases in forty states and handle everything from two-party P.I. matters to environmental coverage claims with dozens of parties. We do a lot of work in the areas of labour and employee-employer relations, construction, real estate, E&O and malpractice, and product liability. I'm especially pleased to include in our materials an insert of the Daily Journal from September 2, 1988, which highlights two articles that I wrote on mediation and its uses.

2. CENTER FOR PUBLIC RESOURCES (CPR)

CPR is one of the oldest ADR organizations, founded in 1979 by James Henry, who chaired the ABA conference on ADR in Toronto. More than 100 law firms are members, and more than half the companies that make up the *Fortune* 500 have signed the "ADR Pledge," a statement that encourages greater use of flexible, creative and constructive dispute-resolving approaches. CPR and its staff are dedicated to spreading the message of ADR to all senior levels of corporate and legal America. CPR also has a few Canadian members.

3. ENDISPUTE, INC.

This is a major ADR supplier, providing a full range of dispute resolution and conflict management services through its offices in Washington, Cambridge and Chicago. It was established by Jonathan Mars and Eric Green, pioneers in a famous process now commonly known as the mini-trial. Endispute's motto is "The best way to resolve a dispute is through the parties themselves." It deals with courts, organizations, corporations, lawyers, etc. Endispute has also prepared a very handy booklet called *Making Alternative Dispute Resolution Work— An Endispute Guide for Practicing Lawyers and Business People.*

4. SOCIETY FOR PROFESSIONALS IN DISPUTE RESOLUTION (SPIDR)

SPIDR, which has mostly mediators, just held its 16th annual conference, "Meeting the Challenges: Professional Dispute Resolution in Changing and Diverse Societies," in Los Angeles, California. The title of the conference indicates some of the wide-ranging ADR topics that will need to be addressed in the future. Bill Kelly, Canada's well-known labour mediator and a governor of the Canadian Institute for Conflict Resolution, is a vice president for SPIDR in Canada.

5. NATIONAL INSTITUTE FOR DISPUTE RESOLUTION (NIDR)

Established as a public foundation to guide and promote the direction of ADR in the United States, NIDR began full operations in 1983. Its mission statement indicates principles of the most important aspects of the ADR movement.

Mission Statement

The purpose of the National Institute for Dispute Resolution is to enhance the fairness, effectiveness and efficiency of the processes through which Americans resolve disputes. Where conflicts serve no social purpose, the Institute seeks out and promotes systematic measures to eliminate the causes of needless controversy. Where disputes do arise, the organization fosters the development, validation, and public acceptance of innovative techniques to resolve them. While respecting each disputant's right of ultimate recourse to formal litigation, the Institute strives to expand the availability and improve the use of alternative procedures with proven capacity to provide more timely, responsive and affordable justice in significant numbers of cases.

The fundamental role of the Institute is to stimulate and assist informed, carefully planned action. Its principal business is to facilitate production of promising ideas drawn from practitioners and from the growing research community, and to translate them into actual improvements in the operation of dispute resolution systems. Positive, real-world change is the primary objective of all Institute activity.

Working directly and through a variety of grantees, collaborators and contractors, the Institute concentrates its resources within four basic categories of effort:

▨ Programs and projects to develop, field-test and document specific methods and policies that offer substantial promise of improving prevention and/or resolution

▨ Assistance to educational and professional institutions as they absorb, analyze, perfect, administer and teach new concepts and techniques.

▨ Support and technical assistance to legislative bodies, judicial conferences, executive departments of government and other officials who are responsible for public policy toward dispute resolution and for the operation of the public agencies and institutions that carry out these policies

▨ Public and professional information programs to broaden and deepen understanding of current events, issues, problems and achievements in the field.

In carrying out all of these activities, the Institute devotes special attention to lessening the dispute-related problems of the poor and other disadvantaged members of society.

Just as positive change is the primary goal of the Institute, the accomplishment of such change is the proper measure of its effectiveness. All Institute programs and projects, both existing and proposed, are evaluated according to their likely contributions to this ultimate objective. Taken as a whole, the work program of the Institute is an agenda for advancing the frontiers of accepted resolution practice, and it is against this demanding standard that the organization assesses the degree to which its mission has been fulfilled.

NIDR has awarded millions of dollars in grants for research, program development, publications and for ADR implementation.

Its progress reports begin with: "The National Institute for Dispute Resolution is a catalyst for innovation and progress in a field that is growing at an extraordinary pace in the 1980's. Citizens in ever-increasing numbers are turning to mediation, arbitration, conciliation and similar methods to resolve conflicts and settle disputes."

NIDR has an extraordinary array of materials and its staff is most cordial.

CANADA

The following organizations are just a few of the ADR organizations that exist. Canada's business and professional communities are only recently becoming more cognizant of ADR, and therefore future developments in Canada in ADR should prove to be increasingly interesting and intense.

I am sure that eventually we will see more law firms develop and expand their ADR services, and joint ventures between law firms and other professional groups that will inevitably lead to multi-disciplinary firms offering problem-solving services to the public.

To help Canadians keep abreast of ADR developments, in spring 1989 there will be a Canadian publication on ADR edited by Professor Paul Emond of Osgoode Hall. This is the type of literature *Without Prejudice* (discussed in Chapter 5) would bring to the attention of its members and discuss at meetings.

1. NETWORK FOR COMMUNITY JUSTICE AND CONFLICT RESOLUTION (RECENTLY RENAMED THE NETWORK: INTERACTION IN CONFLICT RESOLUTION)

This organization is headed by Dean Peachey, who has been an invaluable resource to us. This organization, with a dedicated board of directors that includes many prominent Canadians experienced in this field, publishes a directory of ADR suppliers and organizations across Canada and a quarterly newsletter. It is instrumental in helping others and networking in Canada on ADR matters.

2. JUSTICE INSTITUTE OF BRITISH COLUMBIA

With Marj Berdine at its head, this organization has been very effective in training and has had many ADR successes. Ms. Berdine recently told us of a very successful recent example in which many personal injury cases that were scheduled for trial months and years away were successfully settled within four-hour mediation sessions. Sceptical and reluctant counsel are pleased with the results, as one can imagine, and so are their clients.

Marj Berdine writes:

Located in Vancouver, The Justice Institute's Centre for Conflict Resolution Training provides the most extensive training in the field of mediation in Canada. The Centre offers a Certificate Program comprised of 30 days of training in conflict resolution and two skill assessments. Several thousand students have taken the Centre's training at various locations across Canada over the past six years. Courses are available year round at the Institute or may be contracted to be delivered for private groups and organizations and adapted to meet individualized training needs. Courses are offered in mediation and negotiation skills as well as interpersonal conflict resolution and anger management. The Justice Institute is a provincially funded training centre. The Centre's courses are attended by a wide range of professionals from both private and public sectors.

3. BRITISH COLUMBIA INTERNATIONAL COMMERCIAL ARBITRATION CENTRE (BCICAC)

Established by Bonita J. Thompson, Q.C., its founding director, this centre opened in May 1986. According to information provided by BCICAC, it "was the first such centre in Canada and it continues to lead the way with its facilities and services." Its publication, *Arbitration in Canada* (Vol.1, No.1) boasts: "The Province of British Columbia was the first jurisdiction in the world to introduce the United Nations progressive Model Arbitration Law for international commercial arbitration." It reports in its summer 1988 newsletter that with Ontario having enacted the International Commercial Arbitration Act on June 8, 1988, "every jurisdiction in Canada has now adopted the substance of this United Nations Model Arbitration Law." In the winter 1988 edition it reports that the Quebec National and International Commercial Centre was inaugurated in 1987 in Quebec City. Quebec's legislation was modified to resemble the Model Law of the United Nations Commission on International Trade (UN-CITRAL).

The BCICAC not only provides international services and conferences, but its services are also beneficial to the community. Members of the Vancouver Board of Trade can take advantage of its discounted-fee service for mediation or arbitration to resolve business disputes and personal injury claims. It is also involved in operating as a "network of dispute-resolution organizations to provide efficient, inexpensive and speedy resolutions of commercial disputes among parties trading through the Pacific Rim—the fastest growing trading area in the world."

4. CANADIAN DISPUTE RESOLUTION CORPORATION (CDRC)

According to the principals of this company, CDRC was the first private enterprise ADR service organization in Canada. In business since October 1987, its founder, Brian Gardner, is a Canadian pioneer in the specialized area of delivering ADR commercial mediation services, and has conducted 60 commercial mediations in British Columbia with a success rate of between 85 and 90 per cent. Mr. Gardner's two decades in the insurance industry gave him the experience and insight into the pressing need for alternatives. With the backing of Ed Alfky of Rent-a-Wreck fame, an entrepreneur with a "win-win" attitude and a vision for ADR, the company expects to play a major role. Indeed, CDRC has finalized arrangements with insurance companies to attempt the resolution of up to 600 insurance cases by commercial mediation beginning in the spring of 1989.

5. THE NEMETZ CENTRE FOR DISPUTE RESOLUTION

A banquet in honour of former Chief Justice Nathan Nemetz raised substantial sums of money, which will be applied to help create the Nemetz Centre for Dispute Resolution at the University of British Columbia (UBC). In July 1988 Dean Burns of the Faculty of Law asked Professor Joseph Weiler to prepare a report on the proposed development of this centre. The advisory committee report recommended a plan for the centre to be "an important player in the legal community in British Columbia as well as a leader in the legal education and research field in Canada."

The UBC centre will initially capitalize on cutting-edge collaborative work in substantive legal areas currently going on, and intends to focus on teaching, research and pedagogy in the field of dispute resolution for application in such areas as Asian law, a native Indian program, international trade, labour relations, protection of the environment, constitutional law, family relations, administrative law, and compensation for personal injury cases. A permanent chair will be likely established in dispute resolution. Professor Weiler's research and "conversations with local judges, lawyers, business and trade union people also revealed the same appetite for the new ways to resolve disputes in society."

6. OTHER PRIVATE FORUMS

Similar to the practice in labour matters, there is a growing trend for individuals to offer their services for private arbitration or commercial mediation. Some lawyers are establishing private family law panels to arbitrate family disputes. However, because these arbitrators are practising lawyers, one criticism is the threat to the perception of impartiality based on the volume of usage and ongoing interrelationships on a usual professional basis. Some have expressed concerns about making such panels available for the public if there is an intimacy among its professional users and service providers. Time, market reaction, and empirical studies will help discussion on these points. The Arbitrator's Institute of Canada has long been established in this area.

With the participation of many well-known and respected lawyers, a private court was introduced in Toronto, Ontario in 1988, a Canadian example of what an American journalist described as "a new industry emerging in the shadow of the courts providing private justice for a fee." With more public and professional awareness of ADR, supporters of this alternative should see a wider use of its services. Some judges who applaud this alternative have, however, expressed concern that the use of the word "court" could cause confusion or a perception that this private forum is a type of state-sanctioned court, and have asked for a change in name. The following excerpt is from an eight-page document entitled *The Private Court—How It Works,* prepared by the supporters of this initiative.

Introduction

Litigation today is slow and expensive. In most cases, it is an impractical way to resolve commercial disputes. As a result, there has been a growth of interest in Alternative Dispute Resolution ("ADR"). In the United States, ADR is quite common. The U.S. Centre for Public Resources recently published the following statistic:

> "As of late 1986, more than half the companies that comprise the *Fortune* 500 had signed a pledge saying that they would try to use less expensive, less time-consuming alternatives to litigation in conflicts with each other. More than twenty-five major insurance companies [reported] a similar commitment. In all, companies accounting for more than one quarter of the entire GNP had promised to take all reasonable steps to stay out of court against each other."

According to the information provided by its supporters, the private system has been set up to "establish a practical ADR system in Ontario." Two steps are involved in the process: the first step is a moderated settlement conference, during which an adjudicator attempts to resolve the dispute, and, if that is unsuccessful, the second step is a private trial.

The information says that the aim of this private system is "to remedy the problems faced in the public court system" and to "reduce the overall cost of litigation." The information claims that private systems have reduced the cost of litigation in the United States by 50 per cent through the following means:

a) early and repeated settlement conferences
b) full disclosure
c) early hearings
d) decisions within 30 days
e) flexibility
f) confidentiality
g) informality
h) choice of adjudicator
i) fixed dates

AUSTRALIA

The Australian Conflict Resolution Network, operated by Helena Cornelius and her mother Stella Cornelius, is an exciting example of the grassroots reality and strength of the ADR movement with practical meaning for government bureaucrats, business people, lawyers, and the public at large. In operation for less than two years, the network has more than 30 people who now earn their livelihoods by providing conflict skills training.

Jenny David, a law professor from Sydney, Australia, is about to assume directorship of a second organization, the new Commercial Arbitration Centre. Both Australian organizations publish newsletters about their successes and problems. The September 1988 edition of the Commercial Arbitration Centre's publication, *Resolutions*, carried a story about a Sydney law firm, Westgarth, Baldwich, which has signed a "Declaration of Professional Support" with the Commercial Arbitration Centre, supporting the concept of seeking non-court settlement where possible. According to the newsletter article, the law firm held a conference for about 200 clients entitled "Alternative/New Non-Court Dispute Resolution" conducted by solicitor Ron Finlay, who told his clients that lawyers were problem solvers and that "alternative or non-court dispute resolution offers the business community an opportunity to investigate and participate in dispute-resolution mechanisms..."

8 ADR REPORTS

Any new formula which suddenly emerges in our consciousness has its roots in long trains of thought.
—Oliver Wendell Holmes, *The Autocrat of the Breakfast Table*

IN THIS CHAPTER I present some other reports offering relevant information.

ONTARIO COURTS INQUIRY REPORT
The Honourable T.G. Zuber, 1987

This report by the Honourable T.G. Zuber discusses alternative methods of dispute resolution and offers recommendations. In announcing the inquiry in the Ontario legislature Attorney General Ian Scott explained that the inquiry "…is not intended to be a mere tinkering with the existing system but rather a fundamental rethinking of all the assumptions in which our courts have operated since 1792," in order to "redesign the entire system from the ground up…"

And in a further statement in November 1986 in Winnipeg, Manitoba the Attorney General added:

> …I will expect that [Mr. Justice Zuber] will consider ways of integrating alternative forms of dispute resolution—such as arbitration—as mandatory supplements to the administration of justice in Ontario—an integral and central part of the program.

Some commentators believe that compulsory mediation is an oxymoron. However, the information presented in Chapter 4 seems to demonstrate that ADR processes are limited only by our imagination. As long as the goals of justice are kept in mind, the disputants desire to take more responsibility for the settlement, and fairness, efficiency and affordability are ensured, there must be flexibility for ADR processes to be independent of, adjuncts to, or under the "shadow" of the court.

The Zuber report's findings on ADR are as follows:

Alternative Methods of Dispute Resolution

In recent years, with the increasing cost of litigation and the delays in the court system, many have sought and experimented with other methods of resolving disputes which avoid the need for a trial. In the main, these other methods are simply common sense procedures whereby the parties and their lawyers, or both, are invited or compelled to come together in an informal setting and are then encouraged and assisted to narrow the issues and, if possible, to agree upon a resolution of either part or all of the dispute. These procedures take different forms, such as pre-trial conferences and mediation. Arbitration, although an alternative to trial, is still a method of adjudication rather than a settlement process and will be dealt with separately. Pre-trial conferences and mediation are now used in Ontario. However, the use of these procedures and the success enjoyed varies widely. In some areas, pre-trial conferences are widely used; in other areas, hardly at all. Some judges conduct pre-trial conferences; others do not.

It is the opinion of this Inquiry that the various mechanisms for resolving disputes outside the courtroom should be used to the fullest because they spare the parties very high costs involved in going to court and also the trauma of the trial process. The latter aspect is particularly relevant in family disputes.

It is appropriate, however, to sound a note of caution. Alternative methods of dispute resolution are not cure alls. They do not always work. The procedures should be regarded only as a part of the total package of services offered by the justice system. The courtroom will remain the ultimate method of resolving disputes when other methods have been tried and have failed.

There are a number of reasons why alternative methods of dispute resolution are not more widely used and why they are not more successful. Some judges and lawyers still do not regard these mechanisms as an integral part of the justice system. They are viewed as inherently second class procedures which are not consistent with their expectations as to what competent judges and lawyers should be doing with their time. In short, there is no commitment to these methods as a real alternative. Partially as a consequence of this lack of commitment, the participants do not prepare sufficiently for pre-trial conferences. Judges do not read and fully understand the advance material. Lawyers may be ill-prepared or send juniors who know little or nothing about the case.

Some judges and lawyers are not particularly good at pre-trial conferences and mediation. The traditional skills of trial lawyers and judges may not be sufficient. There are also some weaknesses in the Rule of Civil Procedure and in the legislation dealing with procedures for alternative methods of dispute resolution.

It is the opinion of this Inquiry that steps must be taken to emphasize the concept that, at least in civil cases, resolving issues in the courtroom is the process of last resort and should only be invoked when other methods have been tried and failed. Criminal cases rest on a somewhat sure footing.

Civil cases ordinarily concern only the parties and if they can resolve their disputes privately, no problem arises. In criminal cases, the participants are not just the accused and the prosecution, the public also has a very real interest. Granted that the prosecutor represents the public, but the process of resolving criminal cases requires a quality of openness and a compliance with the appearance of justice that is not present to the same degree in civil cases. However, having said all of that, there are still substantial benefits to be gained in criminal cases by an intelligent process whereby steps can be taken to admit the obvious, narrow the issues and even ascertain that an accused may be prepared to plead guilty to some charge or that the Crown may have a weak case.

An increase in the successful use of alternative methods of dispute resolution can be accomplished only by substantial changes in attitude and by the improvement of skills. The best place to begin this process of change is with the judiciary. **This Inquiry therefore recommends that the judiciary set up seminars and continuing legal education programs with respect to the value and operation of alternative methods of dispute resolution and that, more importantly, these seminars include instruction with respect to the skills necessary to conduct effective pre-trial conferences and mediation hearings** [emphasis added]. It is anticipated that as the judiciary become more expert in pre-trial and mediation procedures, the legal professional will be compelled to follow.

The Zuber report's recommendations on ADR follow:

Alternative Dispute Resolution[1]

108. The judiciary should set up seminars and continuing legal education programs with respect to the value and operation of alternative methods of dispute resolution. The seminars should include instruction with respect to the skills necessary to conduct effective pre-trial conferences and mediation hearings.

109. Pre-trial conferences should be compulsory in the Superior Court and no case should be listed for trial until a pre-trial conference has been held.

110. After the close of the pleadings, any party to a Superior Court action should be able to obtain a pre-trial hearing simply by asking for it.

111. Pre-trial conferences in the Superior Court should be conducted by judges wherever possible.

112. The Provincial Court (Civil Division) rules should be amended to provide that the pre-trial be held before the clerk of the court or referee unless otherwise ordered by a judge; and in that instance, the pre-trial must be conducted by a judge.

113. Suitable instructions should be provided to the clerks and referees of the Civil Division with particular emphasis on consumer protection legislation.

---

1 These recommendations are reprinted by permission of Queen's Printer, Ontario

114. In civil cases in the Provincial Court, a pre-trial should be a prerequisite before a case is listed for trial.

115. The rules for family law cases should be amended to provide that, prior to the commencement of an application, either spouse may request mediation and that, upon receipt of such a request, mediation services will be offered to the parties.

116. The Attorney General should seek an amendment to s.553.1 of the *Criminal Code* to provide that a pre-trial hearing in non-jury cases may be held upon order of the presiding judge, which order may be made upon the application of either crown or defence.

117. The local Courts Management Committee should closely monitor the pre-hearing conference in criminal cases in order to ensure that the process is not abused.

118. A voluntary arbitration mechanism should be built into the justice system. After the commencement of a proceeding, either party should be able to propose that the matter be resolved by arbitration. If the other party or parties agree, and the parties agree upon an arbitrator, the matter should proceed forthwith to arbitration. The arbitration should be a procedure of record and the procedure should accord with the principles of natural justice but the strict rules respecting the admissibility of evidence need not be observed. The arbitration award, when rendered, should be filed with the court in which the matter was commenced and be deemed to be a judgement of that court and appealable as a judgement of that court. The fees of the arbitrator should be paid by the parties to the dispute.

REPORT ON ALTERNATIVE DISPUTE RESOLUTION PROJECTS
Professor Pat Pitsula, 1987

This 76-page study, compiled by Professor Pat Pitsula of Simon Fraser University, a fellow of the CICR, was completed in six months beginning in November 1986. It deals with the "theoretical underpinnings of the ADR movement." Professor Pitsula discusses law-related programs in the U.S. and Canada. Among the U.S. program she includes are the ABA-ADR Special Committee; the Multi-Door Dispute Resolution Program; settlement weeks; programs in Wisconsin, Massachusetts and Colorado; Harvard Law School negotiation projects; and arbitration.

With regards to Canada, she refers to former ABA President William Cox's comments at a 1981 panel discussion, "ADR—Bane or Boom to Attorneys?" in which it was revealed that citizens are not only requesting but also demanding alternative processes. She cites several programs in Canada, including those for family mediation and young offenders, and includes comments from judges and attorneys general in Yukon, Manitoba, Ontario and Saskatchewan.

She discusses some provincial and national organizations, including the B.C. International Commercial Arbitration Centre (BCICAC), whose executive director, Bonita Thompson, is the chairman of the four-person committee of the ADR Special Task Force for the CBA. (See Chapter 7 for more information on the BCICAC.)

The report also discusses U.S. initiatives in elementary and high schools, community neighbourhood justice centres and universities. The report also points out that in Canada the universities' contributions include the work by Professor Andrew Pirie of the University of Victoria, also a fellow of the CICR, who contributed to the paper about ADR in Canada that Mr. Justice Linden delivered to the joint ABA-CBA San Diego meeting on ADR in early 1987. Mr. Linden's paper states that one could safely "speculate that the Canadian legal profession will be a strong supporter of further developments in dispute resolution."

The report reviews community organizations in Canada, deals with peace programs and the Better Business Bureau, and notes that "the field is growing at such an incredible rate." Indeed, I have noticed that those intimately involved in ADR are often unaware of recent developments. Our task is not to slow the tide but to harness the energy.

ADR COMMITTEE FIRST REPORT
Canadian Bar Association—Ontario
May 24, 1988

This report has six parts: goals of dispute resolution, areas and techniques, foreign projects, Canadian experience, choices, and implementation. It discusses "exciting" projects in Canada, including the Woodroffe High School project (discussed in Chapter 9), and says that most discussions about ADR can only be characterized as living history. The report gives an inventory of developments in Canada in the areas of civil law, administrative and labour law, family law, criminal law, environmental law, human rights law, commercial and consumer law, international law, and general law.

FINAL REPORT,
THE CONNECTICUT ADR PROJECT, INC.
1988

The introduction to this report states as follows:

The Problem—General

Since the 1950's our system of justice has been increasingly inundated with civil litigation. There are many reasons for this, including a diminution of our ability to communicate with one another. This reduction is linked to a breakdown in the traditional dispute resolution role in the neighborhood, the family, and religious organizations. Our society has become more complex and we have become more litigious; we call our lawyers to sue before we call our opponents to talk.

As a consequence, the courts have found themselves struggling with increased case loads and inadequate budgets. Inevitably, the courts in many parts of the country have fallen behind; plaintiffs wait years to get their recovery and defense costs have risen dramatically.

The Problems — Particular

Insurers have responded in a variety of ways, both internally and externally, in an effort to find rational and economical methods of handling the rising volume of claims and litigation. Some initiatives, such as their efforts on behalf of torts reform, have met with resistance while others have gained support.

One Solution — The development of ADR

Beginning in the 1970's a number of new organizations began promoting and practicing a promising new form of dispute resolution. This new process became known as ADR: Alternative Dispute Resolution.

In the insurance industry The Travelers was one of the early proponents of ADR as a means of accomplishing both its own objectives as well as those of claimants and their counsel. The Travelers began using ADR in its claim operations in 1983. The reasons for the use of this procedure are:

Voluntary Participation

Parties engage in an ADR process because they understand the advantages of working cooperatively rather than adversarily. There is no contractual obligation to participate. All elements of the procedure are mutually agreed to by the parties.

Flexible Procedure

ADR procedures may be binding or non-binding, brief or lengthy, formal (proceeding under the Rules of Evidence and Procedure) or informal (suspending those rules); may have extensive testimony or limited testimony, etc. To a great extent, the parties create the rules of their own procedure through negotiations.

Timeliness

An ADR procedure generally takes place within one to three months after agreement to proceed.

Cost-Effectiveness

ADR typically costs a fraction of traditional litigation.

Professionalism

In most ADR hearings the parties have the ability to select and agree upon the person serving as the neutral.

The beginnings of the Connecticut ADR project and an analysis of its results were related by George A. McKeon, general counsel for The Travelers Companies, at the 1988 ABA Conference in Toronto:

In late 1985, The Travelers Law Department, Corporate Communications Department and Claim Department initiated the concept of developing a pilot program in Connecticut to explore the potential of the ADR movement. We wanted to know, as did others, whether there were savings to be realized by ADR both in hard dollar and human resources areas and whether ADR could work in large numbers of cases. After considerable efforts were made by Claim and Law Department representatives in contacting senior claim executives of other automobile insurance writers in Connecticut, a top level management decision was made to sponsor the program.

The program began with a meeting in Hartford on July 15, 1986, at which insurance carriers, plaintiff and defence law firms, academicians, and representatives of the Connecticut Judiciary attended, and heard the plans for the coming program. The Travelers provided a grant of $40,000 for the initial development phase, and committed one of our Law Department attorneys to spend whatever time was necessary to have the program operational by the target date of November 1, 1986.

Fourteen insurance carriers committed to submit cases to "The Connecticut ADR Project, Inc." as the program became known. This organization would act as a clearing house, taking in referrals from insurance carriers and plaintiffs' firms and soliciting acceptance from opposing counsel both as to participation in ADR and the type of procedure to be used. Five professional ADR organizations participated as the program's providers, implementing the agreed upon ADR procedure. They were: Dispute Resolution, Inc.; the American Arbitration Association; ADR, Inc.; U.S. Arbitration of Boston; and American Intermediation Service. The project charged a submission fee of $75.00 and, once the case was accepted for a hearing, a $375.00 fee per party. These fees included the charges rendered by hearing officers.

Fourteen months after its inception, The Project had achieved its goal of 1,000 submitted cases and stopped accepting cases on December 15, 1987. Participating companies had grown to twenty-seven and over 10% of the 1037 submitted cases had come from plaintiffs' law firms. The submission of cases The Project received grew from simple, two-party automobile cases to include general liability cases, multi-party disputes and grievous injury and death cases where the settlements reached into the hundreds of thousands and, in one case, over one million dollars.

The success rate of The Connecticut ADR Project exceeded both our expectations and the success rate of our own national ADR program. The Project staff got acceptance to participate from opposing counsel in nearly 80% of submitted cases and *over 90% of cases heard in some type of forum settled as a result of the ADR procedure.* As of this writing, only 25 cases, or 2.5% of the total submitted, were unsettled after hearings while 624 cases, over 60% of the total submitted, have been settled. 180 other cases, 17% of the total submitted, were accepted at the time of this writing and were awaiting scheduling.

Of the 90% of submitted cases which came from insurers, four carriers, Travelers, The Hartford Group, Nationwide, and Liberty Mutual submitted almost half. Eight other carriers submitted between 0 and 5 cases each. This illustrates to us the widely varying degrees of support and management emphasis given to ADR among companies.

Certainly with these results, we feel that...the conclusion that ADR can work is warranted. In our Claim Department program, we have established a target time of 90 days from the date of referral to a provider until the hearing or resolution takes place. In reality, this ends up being in the 150 day range. Our findings on the moderate size case are that the life of that file is reduced by approximately 7 months. Plaintiffs' attorneys who participated in The Connecticut ADR Project indicated on a questionnaire sent out by The Project that they believed their clients saved between 18 and 24 months. Also, Travelers statistics show that we have produced a legal expense saving of $1,000 per case. Since we use staff counsel extensively in our Claim Department litigation, it's reasonable to assume that companies that use outside counsel would experience significantly greater savings.

The real lessons learned, however, come from the cases themselves. The results show that the prompting of the parties by a neutral third party can effect a settlement, even without a formal procedure. The initial contact by one of the project case coordinators often was sufficient to put the settlement process in motion. Secondly, ADR offers a valuable, different way to achieve settlement in cases at impasse. The plaintiff, in many cases, needs someone to hear his/her story. It seems to be irrelevant if the opportunity to tell that story occurs on the witness stand or in a conference room. Immovable and indignant plaintiffs frequently became more amenable to settlement after having an opportunity to relate the nature and severity of the injury or illness to the claim representative and hearing officer. The ability to sit down with an opponent and rationally discuss the case before a mutually selected neutral gives a high probability that the matter will be resolved.

DISCUSSION PAPER: A REFLECTIVE ANALYSIS IN RECONCILIATION AS IT RELATES TO CRIMINAL JUSTICE
National Associations Active in Criminal Justice (NAACJ)
May 6–7, 1987

At the request of the Canadian Department of Justice this paper was distributed to delegates at the international conference, "Reform of the Criminal Law" in London, England in July 1987.

This report highlights the across-the-board challenges to the adversarial process and changes that are manifesting themselves in all areas. Further, given the profound relevance of the criminal justice system to ordinary people, much can be learned from the changes occurring in criminal law: they should remind us how all these events are related, and can also teach us how to deal with conflict when it affects us personally.

The following excerpt from the preamble explains the context and thrust of this paper:

Preamble

This document was first presented at a workshop sponsored by the National Associations Active in Criminal Justice (NAACJ), held in May 1987 in Ottawa, Ontario, Canada. The NAACJ is a coalition of 22 national voluntary organizations in Canada who share an interest in issues related to criminal justice.

This is a time of particular ferment in the work of this coalition because of the historical events that are presently unfolding on the Canadian Criminal Justice scene. The federal government is conducting a fundamental revision of the criminal law in Canadian society. Through the Canadian Sentencing Commission, the Criminal Code Review and the Correctional Law Review, provincial governments and the Canadian people are being asked to re-examine expectations that will affect, for a long time to come, the work of the police, the courts, prisons and parole. At this time as well, our country is contending with a new legislative approach to young offenders that calls for much greater involvement of communities in dealing with crime than has been asked of them in a long time.

There is heightened awareness that adversarial approaches have failed to meet the human need, and that the social sciences alone have failed to deliver on their promises of rehabilitation and crime reduction. There is also a new willingness to move away from incarceration for economic reasons: jails are a luxury the country can no longer afford. At the same time, among the general public, fear and frustrations have been mounting and the question of the death penalty was recently once again brought forward for political discussion.

Member agencies of the NAACJ coalition have been faced for some years now with continuous pressures to respond to government-initiated proposals for reform that are extremely time-consuming, but fragmented and ineffective. The NAACJ has decided that the time has come for the community to take a proactive stand on the more fundamental issues and to prepare itself to deal with crime in a different way. This discussion paper was one of four prepared to assist the associations in their joint exploration of fundamental problems and new directions for criminal justice in Canada.

Another helpful document from NAACJ contains the proceedings of a December 1987 seminar entitled "The Purpose of Criminal Law: Towards a social responsibility model." At the seminar Andrejs Berzins, Crown Attorney for Ottawa-Carleton, opined that a basic problem lies with the adversarial philosophy, and made the following poignant comment: "...especially since the proclamation of the Charter of Rights, *we have moved away from a search for truth*" (emphasis added).

REPORT OF THE CHURCH COUNCIL
ON JUSTICE AND CORRECTIONS
Canadian Sentencing Commission
June 1988

The following excerpt from the report by the CCJC is yet another example of the push for a new paradigm in conflict response and dispute resolution. This movement encourages us to address the fundamental assumptions that we take for granted so that we can redress injustice.

Importance of Paradigm

A paradigm is a way of seeing "the total picture" of an issue, and the meaning of the parts in relation to one another. We change paradigms when new insights make us see the total picture from a different perspective, as in the illustration: the same elements are there but we suddenly see a different set of connections between them and they take on a different meaning in relation to each other and to the whole "gestalt" (what is seen as a vase is now seen as two people face to face).

The Sentencing Commission has done its work within a traditional paradigm of criminal justice. Its work has been done systematically, logically, and comprehensively. It is difficult for any group which works within another paradigm to respond. It is like asking Copernicus to evaluate the work of astronomers who believed the earth was the center of the solar system. He could appreciate their accurate measurements and careful work but his interpretation of their data would have been totally different.

Copernicus could state his new world view simply: the sun is the center of the solar system; after that, everything else fits into place rather simply. The implications, however, were profound.

Copernicus could agree with his fellow astronomers on a number of points: a. it is more important to study the motions of planets taking careful measurements; b. planets move in orbits; c. it is good to be able to predict the motion of the planets. But in spite of this agreement, the conclusions to which the information led him were radically different.

The paradigm of justice which has dominated Western Society goes back to

Roman times. It can be stated simply: crime is the breaking of the law. Justice means to apply equitably similar punishments to fit similar crimes.

CCJC is committed to a different criminal justice paradigm. It can be stated simply as well: crime is harm done to people and the goal of any justice system should be to repair harm done.

Regardless of which paradigm one uses, there are a number of points on which there might be a general agreement: a. the desirability of preventing "crime"; b. the need for community intervention when "crime" is committed; c. the need for study and reflection on "crime" in society. But here too, despite this agreement, the action we might be led to take on the basis of the same information might be radically different.

As will become apparent through this paper, when the studies and observations recorded in the Sentencing Commission Report are interpreted through an alternative perspective, they can be used to substantiate a different paradigm in the same way that Copernicus could use the observations of his fellow astronomers to demonstrate that the sun, rather than the earth was at the center of the solar system. The reason that Copernicus' paradigm was accepted was that people came to see that it was a more valid way of looking at planets.

We are still in the early stages of working out all the implications of the new paradigm. We do, however, have some ideas of what the basic understandings are about. We will present some ideas of what the basic understandings are all about. We will present some of these in the next section and try to show how the contents of the Report of the Sentencing Commission might be viewed through this different perspective leading to quite different conclusions and recommendations.

An Alternate Paradigm

As we try to relate the "new paradigm" to the Sentencing Commission Report, we must first address the question,

"WHAT IS THE OVERALL PURPOSE OF CRIMINAL LAW
IN GENERAL AND SENTENCING IN PARTICULAR?"

It would follow, that one should ask,

"WHAT MORAL PRINCIPLES SHOULD GUIDE THE
CRIMINAL JUSTICE SYSREM AS IT ATTEMPTS TO REACH ITS GOAL?"

In its Spring 1986 newsletter, *Update*, CCJC discussed the Victim Offender Reconciliation Program (VORP), which the CCJC analyzed and recommended in the Report on Sentencing in its March 1988 brief to the House of Commons Standing Committee on Justice. CCJC described the old justice paradigm, which focuses on laws broken, as *assigning blame and punishment*, and the new justice paradigm, which focuses on harm done, as *seeking accountability and restitution*.

The CCJC suggests: "The cornerstone is to centre on the victim-offender-community experience and provide as many opportunities as we can for face-to-face contact that allows us to ground criminal justice work in the human dimension of the reality with which we are dealing."

The report also explains several successful community-based young offender programs. Lorraine Berzins writes: "Central to our ability to begin to do something about violence is owning our own, accepting that we have to learn to mediate and negotiate with each other, and accepting that we are all in this together."

To highlight the convergence of some of these universal principles into a dispute context, I include the following statement from "A Colloquy—Alternative Dispute Resolution in International Trade and Business," part of a symposium on ADR in Canada-United States trade relations held in Maine (a leading jurisdiction in ADR) on May 27, 1987 at the University of Maine School of Law: "Canada in the current trade talks is arguing for a dispute resolution mechanism that is comprehensive, exhaustive of remedies and binding; *in effect a mechanism that institutes restitution not retaliation*" [emphasis added].

REPORT OF THE JUSTICE REFORM COMMISSION:
ACCESS TO JUSTICE
Province of British Columbia, 1988

This report, released in November 1988, is the result of a year's intensive effort. The authors concluded in their covering letter to government: "We sincerely believe that adoption of this report and its recommendations by Government will put British Columbia in the forefront of providing justice services to the public in the most expedient and economical manner possible while preserving the highest standards of justice."

This report's recent release is yet another reminder of how quickly events are unfolding in this area. In the body of the report the committee deals with fundamental questions of the role of litigation, what is ADR, why and when to use ADR, experience in other jurisdictions, whether ADR should be mandatory or voluntary, and the issue of government funding.

The committee's recommendations on ADR are as follows:

Alternative Dispute Resolution[2]

RECOMMENDATION 139
The new Nathan T. Nemetz Centre for Dispute Resolution at the University of British Columbia should conduct the kinds of studies of Canadian ADR projects that have been done in the United States to allow policy-makers to make decisions based on Canadian experience and Canadian values.

---

2 These recommendations are reprinted by permission of the Province of British Columbia, Queen's Printer, and Ministry of the Attorney General

RECOMMENDATION 140

Judges should be encouraged to raise at pre-trial conferences the possibility of referring the issue of the amount of damages, if not liability, to mediation.

RECOMMENDATION 141

The Law Foundation should give careful consideration to funding any proposals for the communication of information about mediation of personal injury claims to the public. If more people are aware of that as an option, more people will insist that their lawyers at least explore the possibility of mediation with them before proceeding with litigation.

RECOMMENDATION 142

The Professional Legal Training Course and Continuing Legal Education should include in their programs information about mediation so that lawyers may become more aware of its availability, particularly in personal injury cases, and its features.

RECOMMENDATION 143

It is the responsibility of every lawyer to consider, at every stage of a lawsuit, those alternative dispute resolution techniques that offer the best prospect of settling the claim and to take advantage of them wherever appropriate. Law schools, Professional Legal Training Course and Continuing Legal Education should emphasize the importance of that responsibility in their courses.

RECOMMENDATION 144

Lawyers who draft contractual agreements should address their minds at that time to the most appropriate means of resolving disputes that may arise, keeping in mind the variety of alternate dispute resolution techniques available.

RECOMMENDATION 145

Every encouragement should be given to community-based projects which provide alternatives to the court system for claims involving small sums of money and appropriate issues.

RECOMMENDATION 146

The centre for alternate dispute resolution at the University of British Columbia should be encouraged to develop a set of standards for training of ADR professionals and to work towards a set of professional standards and a system of certification.

Law Reform Commission of Canada paper
DISPUTE RESOLUTION IN CANADA:
PRESENT STATE, FUTURE DIRECTION
Andrew J. Pirie, April 1987

The author, a professor of law at the University of Victoria and fellow of the CICR, called this 170-page paper a "preliminary consultation paper" and noted that "providing a helpful overview of the present state of dispute resolution in Canada and evaluating potential future directions is a formidable task." The paper covers five parts of disputing processes: description and goal of each disputing process, adjudication by the courts in United States and in Canada; disputing processes in other areas of the law, such as labour, family, criminal, environmental processes, human rights, commercial/consumer; legal and public education in dispute resolution; issues and the future of dispute resolution; and issues and approaches for the Law Reform Commission of Canada.

Professor Pirie states: "there are, in essence, three primary disputing processes: negotiation, mediation and adjudication" which, although "they do not cover the entire disputing field...most other approaches to conflict can be categorized under one of these headings or as a hybrid of them." In addition to analysis in certain specific fields, he suggests that there is a need for researching "foundation information," "goal analysis," the "role of courts and judges in Canadian Society," "cultural connection to dispute resolution," "multidisciplinary teams to gather empirical data," and "fairness" in ADR.

He identifies two models where "dispute resolution processes are commonly applied": a choice model and a linear model. A *choice model*, or "matching a dispute with a process" (using Harvard law professor Frank Sander's multi-door court house concept as an example) is consistent with one purpose of the ADR movement: "to provide greater choices for parties with particular disputes." (See Chapter 1 for a description of Professor Sander's concept.) A *linear model*, "envisages disputes moving from one process to the next, finally ending up, if necessary, in the adjudication process." However, this does not mean all "processes will be tried and exhausted" (i.e., negotiate, mediate, and adjudicate—either by a court or an arbitrator) but rather, "there is a progression from process to process" with "correspondingly higher degree of third party involvement." He critiques these two models and recommends an "integrative model" that "would encourage simultaneous application of various processes to the whole or only part of the dispute." The integrative model does not emphasize choice adjudication, but works on "the presumption that all the disputing processes and their hybrids have the potential to impart benefits to the resolution of a dispute."

As for the goals of ADR, he says that according to the U.S. experience they are acceptable but "whether they are transferable to the Canadian context needs to be addressed." Also, he quite rightly adds that these goals stress the *alternatives* so that "the goals of court adjudication need to be added." This is consistent with my views in this book, that we should consider shifting the popular meaning of ADR from an *alternative to litigation* to an *alternative for people*. (See Chapter 3 for further discussion on the proposed shift in the meaning of ADR.) Pirie also re-emphasizes that the major impetus for ADR in the U.S. was dissatisfaction with the adjudicative process, which is reflected in the described goals of ADR: to relieve court congestion, reduce cost and delay, enhance community involvement, facilitate access to justice and provide more "effective" dispute resolution.

Pirie also responds to the opinion of another writer, who proposed that rather than spending so much effort on alternatives we should apply that energy to improve what we already have in our judicial management of disputes. Pirie's opinion is that we must first come to grips with how we view our courts. He cites a 1984 study by the Council in the Role of the Courts in American Society, which identifies two very distinct ways to view courts: traditionalist and adaptionist.

The traditionalist view is a more rigid, less flexible role where the Court, although fiercely independent, is still dependent on government authority and carries out its functions within strict parameters, almost immune or seemingly unaffected by the human and institutional limitations surrounding the Court in an ever-changing society. This, it seems to me, to impact the role of precedent in the evolution of the law, when and even whether a Court can overrule its previous decisions in a different social milieu.

The adaptionist role looks at the "social firmament" and adjusts to the realities of the evolution of society, and whether or not government legislation politically adapts to the changing times. Some say this is "too broad a repertoire of functions…that require invocation of different processes and different skills by Judges and the administrators that surround them." For the latter approach, precedents can more readily change, and questions are raised whether laws become "judge-made" rather than made by governments. This tension will manifest itself, especially in terms of the application of the *Charter of Rights and Freedoms*. Like everything else, there will need to be a balance, but in the development of jurisprudence, legal scholars and analysts will no doubt notice a pendulum one way or the other.

Essentially, when we accept that our society is guided by the Rule of Law, the challenges are: how does that Rule of Law evolve, is it static (traditionalist) or dynamic (adaptionist), what is the balance in the ADR spectrum of problem-solving between change by government legislation and change by court decisions, and what is the relationship between the judiciary and the government? Such questions are integral to understanding how these principles affect how we conduct ourselves and what processes we use for decision-making.

Mr. Pirie states that although Canadian courts have been more modest in their innovations in dispute adjudication, there have been important changes but there is "great potential" for improvements.

Pirie highlights the areas of ADR principles at work. In the United States these include court-administered arbitration, summary jury trial, early neutral evaluation (ENC), which holds "great promise," managerial judges, and court appeals management plan (CAMP). In Canada they include costs, disclosure, pre-trial conference, judicial blitzing, and the assize system. He warns that conflicts will arise in seeking to achieve the various goals of ADR.

He believes that the ADR movement is in a period of taking stock, with rich ADR experience in the United States and increasingly "more energetic and skilled people in Canada who are committed towards better dispute resolution in Canada." Although Pirie admits that the future of ADR may not be as optimistic as that predicted by Henry H. Perritt, Jr. in his article, "And the Whole World was of One Language," he predicts that "there exists an exciting opportunity to provide input that will actually give direction and form to the processes, laws and values that will significantly affect how Canadians resolve their disputes in the future."

9 INTERNATIONAL AND LOCAL INITIATIVES

Peace and justice are two sides of the same coin.
—President Dwight D. Eisenhower

DISPUTE RESOLUTION CENTRE FOR OTTAWA-CARLETON (DRCOC)/ CENTRE DE RÉSOLUTION DE DISPUTES POUR OTTAWA-CARLETON

Background

The DRCOC was incorporated in early 1987 and received charitable registration status.[1] The board of directors suggested three courses of action:

1. School mediation programs
2. Community boards (neighbourhood justice centres)
3. A national institute to provide the academic resources to meet the needs of DRCOC and other similar groups.

The DRCOC hopes to receive the necessary support from the financial community to carry out its activities.

School Programs

If we are to reach real peace in the world, we shall have to begin with the children.
—Mahatma Gandhi

The DRCOC has developed a good working relationship with the Ottawa Board of Education, and in fact, ADR programs have been established at two schools in the Ottawa Board of Education.

With much joy the DRCOC participated in the first peer mediation program in a Canadian high school at Woodroffe High School in March 1988. Approximately 25 teachers and administrators and 20 students underwent two days of mediation training.

---

1 Because of budget cuts the DRCOC closed its doors in 1999 after 12 years and after handling approximately 2,000 files for minor criminal offences

This program has had many successes. For example, in the words of the school vice-principal, a "donnybrook" was recently avoided, involving almost 40 students from two high schools. Instead of police arrests, juvenile delinquent cases, suspensions, fights and injuries, the combatants resolved the dispute through a mediation session with their school peers.

In addition, the first conflict skills management curriculum in a Canadian elementary school has been launched at Fielding Drive Public School. The entire teaching staff of more than 40 teachers spends one period each week teaching conflict life skills to the 750 students in grades four to eight. Conflict management will soon be added to the curriculum so that children can learn to resolve their own disputes.

Earlier this year the DRCOC made a presentation to the Council of First Nations' education conference in Three Rivers, Quebec. Given the growing use of ADR for Native matters, it was both timely and inspiring for us to be involved with this Native educational conference.

All parents would no doubt be extremely pleased to see such school programs being supported, maintained and expanded. As the ABA has shown in the United States, lawyers can and should play a high-profile public role with business people, educators and parents in ADR. Business people should also be supportive, not only as parents but also as future employers. In fact, the cover story in a recent issue of a major U.S. business magazine was about the CEOs of more than 100 top companies who were involved in "Saving the School" programs that contribute to education skills and attitudes and lead to a more productive workforce. It has been shown that these school programs help reduce vandalism, violence, student suspensions and drop-outs, and teach permanent conflict management life skills that young people can use every day.

As in all things, the school projects will no doubt experience problems, mistakes will be made, and programs may stop or be changed, but patience, perseverance and presence of mind will prevail. The educators and teachers who subscribe to the usefulness of these programs ultimately do the job—all they need is our personal, professional and financial support.

Community Programs

A community board committee of the DRCOC is studying models for communities to resolve disputes between neighbours and therefore avoid relatively minor incidents that can lead to major problems. This initiative would reduce stress on the police, courts, lawyers, municipal politicians, and others. It is hoped that a neighbourhood pilot project will be under way early next year.

CANADIAN INSTITUTE FOR CONFLICT RESOLUTION (CICR)/ INSTITUT CANADIEN POUR LA RÉSOLUTION DES CONFLITS

The CICR was established in early 1988 and received charitable registration status. Its volunteers and part-time professional staff assist the DRCOC in its school programs.

Several eminent persons have already agreed to be governors, and many scholars from various universities have already joined the CICR as fellows with the intent of establishing a national institute for interdisciplinary dialogue and research in conflict resolution. Other intended major objectives include encouraging the expansion of school mediation programs, conducting conflict skills workshops, and providing consulting and educational programs for industries, government, business and professional groups.

The CICR is seeking grants and self-financing programs to achieve its goals.

CONFLICT RESOLUTION DAY OF OTTAWA-CARLETON (CRDOC)/ JOURNÉE DE RÉSOLUTION DES CONFLITS D'OTTAWA-CARLETON

Theme: "Justice is...Just Us"/"La justice, c'est à nous de la faire,"September 29, 1988

This event, involving more than two years of work, was an outstanding evening that achieved very good results. A packed hall of invited guests at the Canadian Government Conference Centre heard eleven speakers from all levels of government and representatives from the legal and educational communities.

With a hard-working committee of nine people and the support of about 50 companies and 50 individuals, we arranged the evening in three months on a budget of $15,000, all donated by government and private sources. The director of the theatre portion said that a program of that breadth would normally take a year to prepare and cost about $100,000.

UNiversal INTERNATIONAL CONFLICT RESOLUTION YEARS (UNICRY): A PROPOSAL

Religious canons, civil laws are cruel—then what should war be?
—William Shakespeare, *Timon of Athens*

We are working on bringing this international initiative to the attention of the federal Minister of External Affairs. I have termed this initiative UNiversal International Conflict Resolution Years, which has the metaphoric acronym UNICRY.[2]

UNICRY has been envisioned as a global movement involving all citizens everywhere working together for this common cause. Individuals, groups, and organizations involved with any aspect of conflict response, dispute resolution and reconciliation programs could all be involved in UNICRY, and this itself would

---

2 UNICRY was originally the acronym for a proposed UN International Conflict Resolution Year but since 1989 has evolved into a broader global movement for all citizens.

further the implementation of communication life-skills and ADR processes—not only individually but also at all levels of government and in all tiers of society.

We believe that at this point in our civilization the principles of peace can be connected in real world ways to the process of peacemaking at all tiers of society, and that Canada is the ideal nation to put this into action, from the interpersonal level to the international level.

It is interesting to note how the public accepts mediation and dispute resolution in high-profile areas such as the UN's role in international disputes and the negotiation of the North American Free Trade Agreement, and even in areas such as labour and family matters. But these methods have not gained general acceptance in legal matters. It is hoped that with education and time we will eventually bridge this comprehension gap; working towards an international initiative like UNICRY could help to that end.

Good contact has been established with the Conflict Resolution Network (CRN), a peace program of the United Nations Association of Australia, whose internationally well-respected principals, Helena Cornelius and her mother Stella Cornelius, are major proponents of this global movement and have supported the vision of using the acronym UNICRY to describe it. It is hoped that other organizations, such as Lawyers for Social Responsibility, will also support the UNICRY concept.

Many people, especially those born in the post-war baby boom, can relate their younger idealism with modern ideals. Among the supporters of conflict resolution matters are various groups and individuals that support so-called peace initiatives but have not been actively involved with them.

The following is a preliminary summary of suggested activities that could form part of the UNICRY global movement:

Schools
Conflict skills curriculums and peer mediation programs.

Communication (Conflict-Resolution) Life Skills
Stella Cornelius has made a written request to the Government of Australia asking it to consider co-sponsoring a UN resolution with Canada for UNICRY. In her submission to the Australian government Ms. Cornelius wrote: "…every written or spoken word that advances UNICRY will further the aims and objectives of our community development program—which is to develop, teach, complement, and learn conflict resolution skills at the international, national, community, or personal levels…we would be immeasurably benefitted by the establishment of UNICRY (and) the process of achieving this will support the work at every turn." She adds: "CRN is preparing a document of conflict resolution initiatives, many at low cost, which can be taken by any country or government, education, business, media, and community organization. This would be a useful reference for UNICRY participants."

Negotiation

UNICRY would bring attention to this essential life skill. In dealing with all types of problems—from interpersonal to international—everyone involved would benefit from learning what it means to negotiate, the importance of perceptions and how negotiation provides long-term gains to everyone involved.

Neighbourhoods

Community boards and neighbourhood justice centres could be introduced for disputes between neighbours or between neighbourhoods.

Culture

Cross-cultural understanding would be enhanced by appreciating attitudinal differences of conflict

Policy

Mediation has been shown to play an important role in public policy issues, at local, provincial and national levels.

Environment

This is becoming a priority issue on the world political agenda, and ADR has been used with some success in the environmental area. UNICRY could provide more focus on how to apply ADR to this critical topic and show how ADR could be used in other important public policy issues.

Universities

UNICRY could encourage the introduction of interdisciplinary dialogue and research, and dispute and conflict resolution studies in the curriculums of all disciplines, especially higher and professional education.

Civil and Criminal Justice

ADR has application in all facets of the law, both the civil (personal) side and the criminal side. It is hoped that UNICRY could encourage more successful criminal justice ADR programs, such as diversion programs, in which the accused is diverted from the criminal justice system, and the Victim-Offender Reconciliation Program (VORP), which brings the victim and offender together with a neutral third party. This type of program is also known as restorative justice, which builds upon Aboriginal teachings and the processes of Aboriginal circles. VORP has been successful because it humanizes the relationship between the offender and the victim, allows the victim to feel more involved in the process, and reduces the recidivism rate.

Business

More businesses are continuing to adopt the use of ADR, both domestically and especially internationally. The commercial potential of ADR is vital to business globally and would greatly benefit from UNICRY.

International

A host of international activities would be relevant and critical dimensions to UNICRY. For example, now is an ideal time for the UN to explain the interconnectedness of interpersonal and international conflict, especially since the UN itself has received recent acclaim for its role in the resolution of conflict between nations, and given that more nations are pursuing non-violent resolutions. UNICRY would also promote the UN's critical role to the world.

Community

The success of the Conflict Resolution Day of Ottawa-Carleton (CRDOC) on September 29, 1988 demonstrated that a great deal can be learned, enjoyed, and promoted with this type of community activity. The theme of the CRDOC was "Justice is...Just Us," and the day's events involved all tiers of society, including youth and all levels of government.

General

Many ideas for an international year can be added to this list by individuals, and organizations such as unions, governments, (*human rights and aboriginal claims*) groups, religious bodies, and professional associations.

An interesting question was recently posed by one of my former law associates, Orm Murphy, managing partner of the Ottawa office of Blaney McMurtry Stapells. Orm has a special familiarity with these ADR issues through his well-known work with the bar and the community as the Official Guardian's representative of children in disputed matters. Orm's question was this: "Where will our world leaders obtain the mandate to resolve international conflict in non-military terms?" It occurred to me that perhaps this would more likely occur when citizens seek to resolve their own interpersonal disputes in non-adversarial terms. UNICRY would allow all peoples to learn about these universal principles and their interrelationships, not just conceptually, but in real terms and in practical ways.

William McMurtry, a partner in the same firm, says that before deciding on a course of action in legal proceedings, he always looks at all the options. Sir Lionel Lukhoo, whom I had the pleasure of meeting a few years ago (and who is named in *The Guinness Book of World Records* as the "world's most successful advocate" with 245 successive murder acquittals) explained a similar methodology: "As a lawyer, my favourite approach in all trials is to clear the decks and examine the status of things and people generally. So let us take a look at the world as it is today."

I agree. Why don't we "take a look at the world as it is today?" Why not encourage looking at all the options, including and within legal (or military) proceedings?

CONCLUSION

War does not determine who is right—only who is left.
—Bertrand Russell

THIS BOOK WILL HAVE ACCOMPLISHED ITS TASK if only one more person discovers the scope of ADR, or applies some of the processes described in these pages, or develops an idea. Perhaps this book will help contribute to the CBA's call for "orderly development" of ADR and assist the CBA's ADR task force. Perhaps there may be something here of interest to the ADR Committee for the Ontario section of the CBA, which I understand has considered establishing a training centre. Or perhaps, just as we have found conferences, literature, and materials that have been helpful, this book may in turn be of some help to others working in or interested in ADR.

But primarily I hope this book is a call for action and contains some ideas that will be actually put into use. When Madame Justice Claire L'Heureux-Dubé of the Supreme Court of Canada made front-page headlines during the CBA Annual Conference in Montreal, Quebec with her comments about the "human" reality of judges and stress on the courts, I realized that one way to relieve stress on the courts is by calling attention to the individual. Individuals can emphasize their role in a dispute only if they are allowed to participate.

Many business people involved in disputes concerned about how the adversarial system hurts a continuing or future business relationship, damages their image in the community, or wastes time, money and people productivity. ADR allows our legal system and our society to address these and other significant issues for our clients, our community, our country and the world.

The opportunities of ADR are unlimited; communication life skills, such as mediation and negotiation, could be taught to all tiers of society; contracts could include "cooling-off" periods and ADR processes; lawyers and business administrators could include dispute resolution as part of their professional mandates, not only for dispute containment but also to ensure that projects get off the ground; judges could apply settlement techniques in addition to their critical adjudicative roles; and legislative changes may result. When the public learns of the remarkable and realistic options available in dispute settlement and conflict resolution, attitudes will change. If we can't eliminate conflict we should try to avoid lawyers, judges, trials, and judgements, or at least try to enlist them to help secure a settlement rather than stretch the strife.

Mr. Justice Linden of the Federal Court of Canada states the case well in the concluding part of his 1984 article, "In Praise of Settlement: The Need for Co-operation":

> The combative spirit has created many problems for our legal system. It has resulted in wasted time and wasted money. It has filled the pockets of some lawyers at the financial and human expense of most litigants. In short, it has brought the administration of justice into disrepute. If nothing is done to halt this trend, the problem will continue to grow. We'll need more judges, more prosecutors, more court houses, and more jails. And we'll have achieved nothing positive in the process.
>
> I believe that we have the ability to halt this trend; we can shift the emphasis of our system to cooperation and conciliation by changing attitudes and by developing new tools. We already have some lawyers and judges who believe that settlement is the better way. What we must do now is convince others of the benefits of cooperation.
>
> Our court system already has developed mechanisms for promoting settlement, but we must broaden the availability of tools such as pre-trial conferences, disclosure, videotaping, codification, costs, and consider new ones, such as the need for leave to try civil cases. At a more basic level, we must strengthen those institutions underlying our legal system which facilitate conciliation, and adjust those which do not.
>
> Canadians, by and large, are a gentle people. We have never been ashamed to compromise our differences. Our entire history is a story of how a diverse people, unlike so many others in the world, has been able to accommodate its rivalries peaceably, without revolution or inordinate civil strife. There are those who feel that this avoidance of confrontation, this willingness to cooperate, is weak, dull, and boring; I do not share that view. To me, a peaceful resolution of a conflict is a glorious triumph for humanity, something that is exciting to behold.
>
> A person shows strength and nobility when, for peace, he gives more than the other person may deserve or accepts less than he feels he is really entitled to. I believe that compromise of this sort, such generosity of spirit, is the truly Canadian way. If this national character trait of cooperation could permeate not only the legal system but the business and political world, it could contribute much to a better world.

In thinking about the matter, I like to apply what I call the "helicopter approach," in which I roam about and carefully view the whole terrain, then land where I want for a closer inspection. If necessary, I can change locations, and sometimes, the helicopter can't properly land. That is one way of treating the subject of ADR when people are looking for the right place to ground their disputes.

A university student once told me that she believed that these days, people don't seek leaders as much as examples. My ten-year-old daughter recently reminded me how lucky I am to have such wonderful children in her and her sixteen-year-old brother! I responded by confessing how I am coming to see that everything I know about faith and love I am learning from my children. She unhesitatingly responded by saying: "I can understand that; you teach us about those things and then you have to be an example."

As has been so widely said, example is the best philosophy. If we can overcome whatever stops us from applying these simple truths to our livelihoods, then we will be in a better position to work out our differences. My son queried, why do people make artificial distinctions, in his words, between "work" and "volunteerism," which could result in differing and contradictory principles being lived out? It made me think of the famous line from a movie, which the hired killer utters just before the murder: "Don't take it personally, it's only business!"

Lawyers, by assuming their professional mandate as advocates and not adversaries, can play an increasing role in the broad range of conflict issues facing our world. But lawyers, like everyone else, are expected to not only help explain but also to exemplify these principles in practice. The good news, though, is that those of us who are involved in the administration of justice, whether as lawyers, judges, public servants or otherwise, need not take this focused reconsideration of the role of the adversary system personally since it seems to be only part of an overall re-evaluation of all of the basic assumptions in our social structures.

For example, the true, apparently often misconstrued philosophy of the mysterious Chinese warrior-philosopher Sun Tzu is the classic stated goal: "To win without fighting is best." And to win is meant not in an unrelated sense, but in the sense of finding mutual problem solving, as explained in the 1988 book, *The Art of War: Sun Tzu*, by Thomas Cleary, a scholar of Taoism and Sun Tzu:

> The healing arts and the martial arts may be a world apart in ordinary usage, but they are parallel in several senses: in recognizing...that the less needed, the better; in the sense that both involve strategy in dealing with disharmony; and in a sense that in both, knowledge of the problem is key to the solution.

Cleary elaborates that "the art of war applies to competition and conflict in general, on every level from the interpersonal to the international"; it ultimately seeks to teach that "...the peak efficiency of knowledge and strategy is to make conflict altogether unnecessary."

Our hope to achieve this will be through understanding change through education. As Griffiths and Polanyi wrote in *The Dangers of Nuclear War*:

> If we survive, it will be because we have harnessed these same forces of techno-logical change and of improved education to the task of bringing ourselves and our fellows to an appreciation of a changed world.

According to Mr. Justice John Sopinka of the Supreme Court of Canada, the legal profession is a most valuable asset in working at this change. But to achieve change, lawyers must be more than mere tacticians and technicians, otherwise they could be seen as a wasted asset.

Leonard Riskin's excellent article, "Mediation and Lawyers," says that the obstacles to mediation are the lawyer's philosophical map and "mental grooves and compartments." While he acknowledges the positive aspects of the tra-ditional legal system and lawyers' conventional wisdom, he also points out how it "permits a great deal of misery." He first explains in very practical terms why a lawyer should not perceive ADR and mediation as economic threats but rather as financial boons, and then he states: "Though the preceding argument may not dispel worries about lawyers' financial security, 'higher' perspectives in jurisprudence, in the orientations of individual lawyers and the bar and in the goals of legal education, can pull the legal profession toward appropriate and deeper involvement with mediation." He says these aspects do much to "improve the quality of life in our society," but if not embraced, he warns that they could be a repellent to the future profession.

Unless lawyers, as a profession, adopt an upward sense of our role in soci-ety, then we will see a gradual downward spiralling of our collective contri-bution and participation in the changes emerging in response to conflict and the resolution of disputes. John Kelly, Chair of the ADR Committee for the Canadian Bar Association—Ontario says that we should look at the calibre of what is being said by whom. But if the public perception is that the only incen-tive of lawyers in mediation and arbitration is to protect their own economic self-interests, such efforts could be fraught with danger. As a senior and high-ly respected member of the Ontario Bar, John Nelligan of Nelligan Power, so astutely put it: "We don't have to put another red cent into our court system to improve access to justice—we just have to change our attitude." The pro-posed UNICRY movement may assist in focusing our attention on this change of attitude.

Gordon Henderson, another senior member of the Ontario Bar and author of the foreword to this book, once said that when we realize that we are all captured by the circumstances of our birth, times, and geography, we then have a chance to not only escape and free ourselves from the trap of our restricted thinking but also to share our collective experiences. The choice (indeed, the responsibility) is ours.

But why don't we do this? One story that may shed some light on the answer involves a turtle and a scorpion. The scorpion asked the turtle to carry him on his back across the stream. The turtle refused, explaining that he feared the scorpion would sting him and he'd die. The scorpion countered by saying said that would be illogical because if the turtle died he'd end up drowning. The turtle was convinced of this argument and agreed to the scorpion's request. Halfway across, the scorpion stung the turtle. As they were both sinking beneath the water, the turtle turned its head and said to the scorpion, "You said it would be illogical to sting me since you knew we'd both drown! So why did you do it?" The scorpion's reply: "It has nothing to do with logic. It's just my nature."

Is it our nature to seek our own self-destruction?

Not long ago I had a memorable lunch with Professor John Sigler, of Carleton University's Political Science Department, who is especially recognized for his expertise in Middle Eastern matters. When the suggestion was made during lunch that we are bent towards mutually assured destruction (MAD) because it is in our nature, Professor Sigler pointedly remarked, "Not so—it is in our culture." This thought for me was most provocative and enlightening, and actually made me feel more hopeful about our ability to resolve disputes without the excuse of our nature being in the way.

In the continuing search for understanding I subsequently came upon a thought attributed to Gandhi, who had written in a private note: "...there is something in man which is superior to the brute nature in him..."

Gandhi is known to have been inspired by the great Russian writer Tolstoy, who once wrote Gandhi a personal letter in which he referred to the contradictions of those who profess peace but practice violence through the "power of rulers, courts and armies." I recall a comment made by an anthropologist at a conference, that in non-Western cultures, it is litigation that is considered ADR!

So where do we start? I remember when the Dispute Resolution Centre for Ottawa-Carleton first contacted the Ottawa Board of Education about pioneering Canada's first peer mediation high school project (described in Chapter 9). Charlotte Lemieux, the Director of Education at the time, responded warmly and gently and without hesitation: "If we are to achieve the ultimate goal of world peace then we have to start with our children."

And where do we end? I am reminded of the story of the ancient emperor whose troops were noisily preparing to celebrate their historic victory. He admonished them for their celebrations, telling them that they had yet to win the greatest battle of all. And what battle was that, they asked? His response: "For inner peace, through the battle within."

In the end, it seems that literature and life experience speak of the interconnectedness of things; whether the dispute, therefore, is headed towards the battlefield of the military or of the courtroom, and whether it concerns an interpersonal or an international matter, it is more important to solve the problem without fighting than to devise the rules for the battle.

Hence, we could miss the meaning and promise of the conflict topic if we insist on remaining myopic!

"But wait a bit," the Oysters said, "before we have our chat."[1]

The reality seems to be that there's no putting off dealing with ADR and we are urged to 'chat' about the lawyer's role in these principles and process-es. This will involve some retooling, which is typical of our modern age, but it is an exhilarating breakthrough for the practice of law, and the use of and expansion of lawyers' skills. At the same time, the legal profession can also break through other barriers. Lawyers can work with non-lawyers involved in ADR services, and by dealing with the "whole paradigm" approach discussed in this book. There can also be a breakthrough with the lawyers' image bar-rier. We can provide better service to our clients only when we truly serve them.

"The time has come," the Walrus said, "to talk of many things."[2]

Now that our minds did wrap around ADR, whose terrain we did roam, please let me wrap up by way of a poem:

If our world is like a symphony, a homogenous substance,
    it is thus our goal,
To understand that the voice of each particle is unique and separate,
    but reflective of the whole.
Let us therefore take a threefold vision to sound out of these matters
    their heart and soul;
First, a telescope to view the universal pole,
Next, binoculars to watch each group troll,
And, finally, a microscope to measure each individual's role.
Then we see that we are at once different but also the same,
As the wise man once said, each a spark from a common flame.

It is hoped that our efforts, programs and this book have
    with you found favour:
They're akin to giving birth: easy to conceive, hard to deliver,
    but well worth the labour!

At the outset acknowledgements were extended,
Preceded by a sculpture described in a page;

---

1   Lewis Carroll, *Through the Looking-Glass*

2   *Ibid*

The introduction sought to have blended,
The various approaches to be taken, guided by a sage.

Our two years' experience was revealed that took us so far;
Conferences, organizations, and reports we did explain;
The history in brief, with concerns, were excerpted about ADR,
And why, it seems clear, dispute resolution will now
    never be the same.

A new meaning was suggested for ADR the acronym,
As "alternatives for people" and not "alternatives to court;"
So, while we disengage from "win-lose" to "win-win,"
We don't, any options, conciliating or contentious, thwart.

We then looked at what other well-known people did say,
About why we should find alternatives to handle our strife,
Suggesting a national program "Without Prejudice,"
    for lawyers and business people as an appropriate way,
To get on with our problem solving and enjoy a better life,

But, the words "attitude, law, justice, ADR, win-win, win-lose,"
    and any other alleged truths,
Mean little unless we can mount,
Programs and processes for people to use,
Because, in the world, it is our actions that count.
    —Ernie the Attorney

APPENDICES

APPENDIX A

THE DISPUTE RESOLUTION CONTINUUM

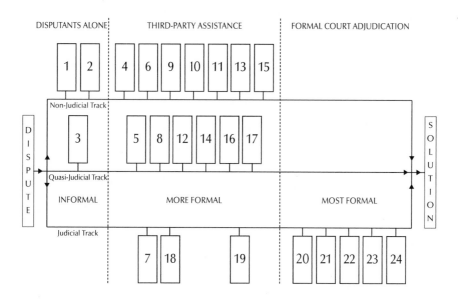

LEGEND

1 Negotiation (Unstructured)
2 Negotiation (Structured)
3 Rent-A-Court
4 Expert/Fact-Finder (Non-Binding)
5 Consult-A-Judge
6 Private Conciliation/Mediation
  (Non-Binding)
7 Multi-Door Court
8 Court-Annexed Conciliation/Mediation
9 Expert/Fact-Finder (Binding)
10 Private Mediation (Binding)
11 Arbitration
12 Court-Annexed Arbitration

13 Private Jury
14 Court-Annexed Summary
   Jury Trial
15 Private Mini-Trial
16 Court-Annexed Mini-Trial
17 Rent-A-Judge
18 Drive-Through Filing
19 Pre-Trial Conference
20 Night/Weekend Court
21 Simplified Trial
22 Master/Expert
23 Special Complex Litigation
24 Procedures

APPENDIX B

OTHER QUESTIONS TO PONDER

A book that furnishes no quotations is, me judice, no book—it is a play thing.
—Thomas Love Peacock, *Crotchet Castle*

A Better Way

If it remains true that conflict is the universal predicament of nature and mankind, nevertheless it seems as if we are beginning to discover that cooperative resolution to conflict touches upon an equally universal principle.

  —Professors Douglas Wurtele and Kenneth Melchin

A common thread pervades all courtroom contests: Lawyers are competitors and once litigation begins they strive mightily to win using every tactic available. Business executives are also competitors, and when they are in litigation, they often transfer their normal productive and constructive drives into the adversary contest. Commercial litigation takes business executives and their staffs away from the creative paths of development and production and often inflicts more wear and tear on them than the most difficult business problem...The plaintive cry of many frustrated litigants echoes what Learned Hand implied: "There must be a better way."

  —Chief Justice Warren E. Burger

Most disputes involving legal rights and obligations are not litigated in court at all. They are settled more or less amicably between parties, with or without lawyers or other advisors. When lawyers (or other advisors with some knowledge of the law) are involved in attempting to settle such disputes, they rely upon judicial precedents in the same way that lawyers do in court.

  —P.S. Atiyah

Dr. Pierre Hurtubise, Rector of St. Paul University, whose field of specialty is Italian history, recounted an anecdote from a symposium in Italy: At the collapse of the Roman Empire, because of the chaos of the legal system the citizens organized their own system of justice in which an aggrieved party could slap the face of a common law tortfeasor in public. (Would a modern-day application be possible?)

The following quotes appear in the pamphlet "Alternative Dispute Resolution—an ADR Primer," printed by the American Bar Association:

Discourage litigation. Persuade your neighbors to compromise whenever you can. Point out to them how the nominal winner is often the real loser in fees, expenses and a waste of time.

—Abraham Lincoln

People with problems, like people with pain, want relief, and they want it as quickly and inexpensively as possible.

—Chief Justice Warren E. Burger

The courts of this country should not be the places where the resolution of disputes begin. They should be the places where disputes end—after alternative methods of resolving disputes have been considered and tried. The courts of our various jurisdictions have been called "the courts of last resort."

—Justice Sandra Day O'Connor

Litigation is approaching a new horizon, a new dawn, and when we get there the change will be from that of seeking justice through attack, battles, and champions to the constructive, tolerant disposition of controversy...for enduring public standards of equity and justice.

—Eugene C. Thomas

From *Arbitration Canada,* the news publication of the British Columbia International Commercial Arbitration Centre:

The logo of the British Columbia International Commercial Arbitration Centre symbolizes the orderly process of diffusing disputes through mutual and co-operative effort—moving from fixed and uncompromising positions of conflict to a harmonious and productive resolution.

—Vol. 1, No. 1

There is after all an element of truth to the old adage that slow justice is no better than speedy injustice. Lengthy delays in civil cases favour affluent litigants over those of more modest means. Delay distorts the financial effects of the ultimate verdict on the parties and may impose severe emotional strains...Perhaps an...answer is to be found in the increased use of arbitration and mediation instead of litigation in civil matters.

—Honourable Brian Dickson, Chief Justice, Supreme Court of Canada

Arbitration is a method of dispute settlement that draws on the finest traditions of compromise and respect for the rule of law: principles upon which not only commercial relations are built but nations as well.

—Honourable Ray Hnatyshyn, Minister of Justice, Vol. 1 No. 1

Nobody wins from litigation. The cost of winning disputes for our clients, whether in Canada or abroad, has been enormous. Every business person, every industry, is crying for effective alternative dispute resolution.

—David Pym, President, International Risk Management Ltd.

Services supporting alternative dispute resolution—such as arbitration and mediation—point out the path we must follow. They are fast, effective and inexpensive. They have earned the trust and confidence of those who have used them. They have gained momentum. And they are here to stay.

—Jean Bazin, President, Canadian Bar Association, Winter 1988

Ordinary people have lost patience with the justice system. They feel alienated from a system that is too complicated, too expensive and far too slow.

—Brian Smith, Attorney General of British Columbia, Winter 1988

The mediation process—which is conciliatory and voluntary—offers an attractive alternative to business people from cultures where final adjudication of a dispute is considered most unsatisfactory.

—Bonita Thompson, Winter 1988

Everyone talks today of mechanisms for alternative dispute resolution; here is just such a mechanism; that scheme should be allowed to flourish.

—Madame Justice Prinafort, Supreme Court of British Columbia,
in upholding an arbitrative award, Winter 1988

But, on the other hand, there is this reminder:

It should also be recognized that in many cases the court is sometimes the only protection the weak and the timid have against stubborn and unreasonable adversaries. We must all be careful not to let that important responsibility be transferred to other disciplines whose remedy (often ineffectual) is reasonable persuasion.

—Allen McEachern, C.J.B.C., in a speech delivered at the Canada/U.S. Legal Exchange, 1987
(quoted in the *Access to Justice* report to the Province of British Columbia., November 1988)

THE BUSINESS ANGLE

As a businessman, if I don't listen to the market, I'm not in business. If I were an attorney, I'd make sure I was involved in alternative dispute resolution, because it may well be the service that the market will demand and I'll have to offer in the future.

—Walter Wriston

Probably the most important management fundamental that is being ignored today is staying close to the customer to satisfy his needs and anticipate his wants.

—Lew Young, Editor in Chief, *Businessweek*

The excellent companies are the listeners...most of this real motivation comes from the market.

—Peters and Waterman, *In Search of Excellence: Lessons from America's Best-Run Companies*

The best companies are pushed around by their customers.

—*Ibid*

The fluidity of business is simply too fast and too formless for existing systems and structures to hold it. But good management must resist both the internal and external pressures to force new business into the old holes, simply because those holes already exist. Once a company allows structure to run its operation, it is only a few missed opportunities from total stagnation.

—Mark McCormick, *What They Don't Teach You at Harvard Business School*

Managing a mature company is not just a constant process of breaking out of archaic structures and antiquated policies. You also have to be consciously, actively and aggressively punching holes in the company's conventions and wisdom. It's too easy to say, "It's worked this way before," or "That's how we've always done it." It's too easy to get mentally locked in, to reject automatically a fresh or new approach.

—*Ibid*

Where the pleasure comes in my practice is in being innovative…you always thing of new ways to achieve the client's objective.

—Paul Moore, quoted in Jack Batten, *Lawyers*

Statements of satisfaction with ADR process, from one of the parties and one of the neutrals in the $833 million IBM-Fujitsu software-infringement dispute. (*Alternatives*, November 1987 and January 1988):

Fujitsu is very pleased with the resolution of the disputes between Fujitsu and IBM. The resolution of these disputes fulfills Fujitsu's desire to have rivalry with IBM returned to its natural and appropriate arena—the marketplace.

—Fujitsu Ltd.

We think that this conclusion is what dispute resolution should be all about: the prompt creation for fair and just outcomes that recognize both parties' rights, obligations and interests.

—Robert Mnookin, Mediator, Center for Public Resources, New York

ATTITUDE CHANGES AND LEARNING

We don't have to add a red cent to our court system to improve access to justice—we just have to change our attitude.

—John Nelligan, law firm of Nelligan, Power in Ottawa

Most of the time we don't communicate; we just take turns talking.

—Dr. Robert Anthony, *Think*

There is probably nothing in this book which you did not already know at some level of your experience. What we have tried to do is organize common sense and common experience in a way that provides a usable framework for thinking and acting.

—Fisher and Ury, *Getting to Yes*

Principled negotiation produces wise agreements amicably and efficiently.

—*Ibid*

It is not easy to change habits.

—*Ibid*

Are you married? Who's winning?

—*Ibid*

...fundamental changes are necessary, not only in our economic and political structures, but also in our values, in our concept of man's aims, and in our personal conduct.

—Eric Fromm, *The Anatomy of Human Destructiveness*

In the following pages, I offer nothing more than simple facts, plain arguments and common sense; and have no other preliminaries to settle with the reader than that he will divest himself of prejudice and progression and suffer his reason and his feelings to determine for themselves.

—Thomas Paine, *Common Sense*

Loving peace is not enough. We also need a peacemaking vision, science, strategy and action.

—Robert Mueller, *A Planet of Hope*

Our destination is never a place but rather a new way of looking at things.

—Henry Miller

Into the conflict will come a new mood, a new attitude—not a new law nor a new contract.

—John Howard Yoder, *He Came Preaching Peace*

It is my contention that—despite all of the vicissitudes and stuff—an objective analysis of the facts [indicates] that humankind is experiencing an erratic and turbulent evolution towards rational world order.

—Benjamin Ferencz, *A Common Sense Guide to World Peace*

I share (the) optimism in believing that, being an institution, war can be abolished.

—Konrad Lorenz, *On Aggression*

Life need not become static at the dead-point, the point arrested development, where habit, custom—all that makes up "law"—becomes too heavy, and where growth is stifled under a nerveless hand.

—R.C. Mowat, *Climax of History*

But remember that you are marching into this battle to the beat of a different drum. It is a battle to change the rules of human communication. We cannot change the rules through playing the old ones.

—M. Scott Peck, *The Different Drum*

The dogmas of the quiet past are inadequate in the stormy present. We must think and act anew.

—Abraham Lincoln

All truth passes through three stages: First, it is ridiculed; second, it is violently opposed; third, it is accepted as being self-evident.

—Arthur Schopenhaur

Social existence is a continuing process: as one of its problems is solved, others emerge, often from the previous solutions themselves. Our habit is to ask for solutions. The very best ones will be only a temporary achievement, although nobody should minimize the importance of that.

—John Kenneth Galbraith, *The Age of Uncertainty*

Down to Gehenna or up to the Throne, He travels fastest who travels alone.

—Rudyard Kipling, *The Story of Gadsby*

[There are] processes of life carried on by long-established and well-defined classes [such as] lawyers...all with time-sanctioned codes. Now wholesale reclassification, representation of humanity to a new, vaster, richer and more satisfying set of objectives has to be taken strenuously and immediately.

—H.G. Wells, *The Outline of History*

For decades critics of the litigation system have bemoaned the delays and costs of courtroom encounters while working mightily to refine the system in ways that make it even slower and more expensive. This paradoxical approach reflects the strengths and weaknesses of legal training. Skillful in analysis and advocacy, lawyers have recognized those aspects of trial procedure that can be changed to increase the likelihood of achieving better results and then engrafted well-intentioned changes onto an already complex system. At the same time, lawyers' preoccupation with results and their inadequate appreciation of the need to evaluate the system in which they function cause them to ignore the adverse consequences of the litigation process they have constructed. They know that the system is slow and costly. But they fail to recognize that the solutions they have developed over the years are a large part of the problem.

—John Newman, *Rethinking Fairness: Perspectives on the Litigation Process*

The contribution of the lawyer to redistributive social change, then, depends upon the organization and culture of the legal profession. We have surmised that court-produced substantive rule-change is unlikely in itself to be a determinative element in producing tangible redistribution of benefits. The leverage provided by litigation depends on its strategic combination with inputs at other levels. The question then is whether the organization of the profession permits lawyers to develop and employ skills at these other levels. The more that lawyers view themselves exclusively as courtroom advocates and the less their willingness to undertake new tasks and form enduring alliances with clients and operate in forums other than courts, the less likely they are to serve as agents of redistributive change.

—Mark Galantery,
Why the Haves Come Out Ahead: Speculation on the Limits of Legal Change

...both were happy over the result, and both rose in public estimation. My joy was boundless. I had learnt the true practice of law. I had learnt to find the better side of human nature to enter men's hearts. I realized that the true function of a lawyer was to unite parties riven asunder.

—Mahatma Gandhi, *The Story of My Experiments With Truth*

SOCIOLOGY OF THE LAW

The lawyer, as a practical man of the world, has tended, especially in common law countries, to be somewhat impatient of theory and to adopt the attitude that this task is to solve practical problems and that for this purpose he is better quipped by virtue of his legal experience than those who, however well versed in other disciplines, lack his grasp of legal essentials. In the last resort, however, the claims of the social sciences to be heard, even in the arcane of the law itself, must depend both on the light they can be shown to shed upon legal institutions and assistance they can render in the solution of the actual legal problems of one day and age...thus impact upon legal thinking and practice has already proved to be considerable, and the legal sociologist is presented with an immense field for research, much of which remains virtually unexplored.

—Denis Lloyd, *The Idea of Law*

IMPERFECTION AND THE INDIVIDUAL'S ROLE

No doubt by oversight God did not declare the judicial mind to be an error-filled zone. Even if error is not conceived at trial, the rhythm of appeals guarantees continuing futility.

—Justice John Scollin, quoted in *Legal Wit and Whimsy*

Making law is not always the same as making sense.

—*Ibid*

Notwithstanding its transcendent and long-standing popularity, the rule of law has been under mounting pressure in modern society...against a backdrop of lawlessness and social frustrations certain [events] reveal the extent of popular dissatisfaction with the legal and established order... for the process, the legal system itself has become a form of dissent.

—Hutchinson and Monahan, *The Rule of Law: Ideal or Ideology*

In all law there is, and nothing can avoid it, a conflict as unending as the war between Heaven and Hell, a war between two principles that may never be reconciled but only compromised. On the one hand there is the principle (said by some to be a high principle): *fiat justitia ruat caelum* ("Let right be done, though the Heavens should fall"); on the other hand there is the pragmatism (said by others to be low and unworthy): *interest republicae ut sit finis litium* ("It concerns the state that there be an end to lawsuits," or "It is for the general welfare that a period be put to litigation." *Black's Law Dictionary*, 4th ed., 1968) And so the conflict may not cease because whilst there are lawsuits there will be defeated litigants, and whilst there are defeated litigants, the clamour for the application of the high principle will never be stilled. The low pragmatism may interest the republic but it interests the defeated litigant not at all. Is this of Heaven or of Hell?

—Allan C. Hutchinson, *The Formal and Informal Schemes of the Civil Justice System: A Legal Symbiosis Explored*

As in every generation there [were] attorneys and judges whose clear and disciplined minds were at the service of truth and justice regardless of fee; and the lowest practitioners were redeemed by the great jurists whose names are the highest in the history of the law.

—Will Durant, *The Roman Empire*

He will ever bear in mind that if he be the advocate of the individual, and retained and remunerated (often inadequately) for his valuable services, yet he has a prior and perpetual retainer on behalf of truth and justice.

—Mr. Justice Crampton, 1844

In the last analysis, the administration of justice is done by people and it is the character and quality of the people, whether they be judges or advocates which are the controlling factors.

—J.J. Robinette, *Ontario Lawyers' Weekly*, July 8, 1983

Our legal systems must attempt to respond to the legitimate needs of our complex society. To respond the system must, of necessity, be reasonably affordable, accessible, comprehensible, and capable of resolving conflicts in a timely fashion. Otherwise it will not foster the confidence and respect that it must have to function effectively...

—Rene A. Stradiotto, President, Advocates Society of Ontario

Alternative forms of dispute resolution can be a valuable adjunct to the judicial system, but the judicial system must remain the effective, final forum for the determination of people's rights.

—*Ibid*

DISLIKE OF THE LEGAL SYSTEM

The first thing we do, let's kill all the lawyers.

—Shakespeare, *Henry VI*

Why does a hearse horse snicker hauling a lawyer away?

—Carl Sandburg, *The Lawyers Know Too Much*

As litigant, I should dread a lawsuit beyond almost anything short of sickness and death.

—Learned Hand, U.S. judge and judicial philosopher

Out of the many lawyers so trained there were inevitably some who sold their learn-ing to sordid causes, accepted bribes to present their clients' case weakly, found loop-holes in the law for any crime, fomented disputes among rich men, dragged on suits to any lucrative length, and shook the courts or the Forum with his intimidating ques-tioning and vituperative summations.

—Will Durant, *The Roman Empire*

Gandhi's law practice was based on the proposition that "settlements out of court were preferable to trials" and [he] "disliked the competitiveness of lawyers."

—Louis Fischer, *The Life of Mahatma Gandhi*

Only a small percentage of today's mesmerized populace is aware of the fact that the legalman in the course of his work can say virtually anything he pleases both in legal briefs and in the courtroom. He can make wild accusations and dispense totally false information without fear of fine or punishment.

—Robert Ringer, *How You Find Happiness During the Collapse of Western Civilization*

We practice law to make money; however, if you know a more compelling reason to practice law, let's hear it.

—D.R. White, *The Official Lawyer's Handbook*

Litigators are proceduralists. They are less concerned about who gets beheaded than about whether the guillotine is well oiled and running smoothly.

—*Ibid*

The adversarial system rests on the curious promise that out of the clash of lies, truth will emerge.

—*Ibid*

The amazing thing is that litigators are unembarrassed by this role...a lot of young lawyers get sucked into litigation because that's all law school has really taught them to do. Sadly, a number of perfectly nice people, fully capable of being embarrassed, end up as litigators.

—*Ibid*

Cartoon: A little advice...Practice the courage of your convictions outside the office.

—*Ibid*

Legal ethics come down to one word—money. Fairness, kindness, a commitment to helping people resolve their own disputes are all irrelevant.

—Warner and Ihara, *29 Reasons Not to Go to Law School*

Tell a lawyer today you've just worked out a scheme that will establish justice, promote domestic tranquility and ensure general welfare, and he'll end up persuading you that if you're lucky and carefully follow his advice you may end up not going to jail.

—*Ibid*

...not for frogs nor gnats, flies nor boils, hail nor locusts, persuaded Pharaoh to let the children of Israel go. It is foolhardy to question divine wisdom, but is at least arguable that somewhere between gnats and locusts, and surely before the death of the first-born shattered Pharaoh's stubborn resolve, a plague of lawyers would have been enough.

—Jerold S. Auerbach, quoted in Pirie, *The Lawyer as Mediator*

Justice by its very definition belongs, *a priori*, on one side or another, or so we tend to believe; but it may be independent of the final result. We have, furthermore, construed statutory and constitutional mandates to require "fairness" in the battle process of our adversary system. In a fair game, the opponents are both assumed to be entitled to win if they can. The win-lose adversary situation thus creates the following dilemma:

> Justice is on one side only. But one must fight for one's own side. Moreover, one must fight as hard as one can, using all the tricks of the trade, as long as the rules are obeyed. But what it justice is on the other side?

And one may add, what if justice is on neither side? What if neither is at fault?

—James Marshall, *Lawyers, Truth and the Zero Sum Game*

Given the zero-sum situation, the lawyer enters the courtrooms with his energies channeled toward the goal of "winning his case." Thus, while the adversary system may be a form of dialogue that winnows the evidence and clarifies, the system unfortunately, leads to the psychological drive for victory and the drive for victory is, in essence, a power drive. This, in turn, tempts the seeker of victory to use weapons of power that have little relevance to the purpose of a judicial system to administer equal justice. Distortion (if not misrepresentation) and the manipulation of bias defeat the possibility of finding truth or reality. Thus the adversary system is often used not as a means to equal justice, but as a technique for victory.

—*Ibid*

Hardly a day goes by that we do not hear or read of the dramatic increase in the number of lawsuits filed, or the latest multimillion-dollar verdict, or of another small business, child care center, or municipal corporation that has had its insurance cancelled out from under it.

—Senator McConnell, quoted in Galanter, *After the Litigation Explosion*

Across the country, people are suing one another with abandon; courts are clogged with litigation; lawyers are burdening the populace with legal bills... This massive mushrooming litigation has caused horrendous ruptures and dislocations at a flabbergasting cost to the nation.

—Columnist Jack Anderson (publication and date unknown)

Everybody in the U.S.A. suddenly seems to want to sue anybody with liability insurance coverage. The explosion of litigation has choked our court dockets. And too few lawyers tell potential clients that some cases are a waste of time. The greed has turned the temple of justice, long a hallowed place, into a pigsty. The time has come to clean it up."

—USA Today (writer and date unknown)

The Aetna Insurance Company tells us that "America's civil liability system has gone berserk....[It] is no longer fair. It's no longer efficient. And it's no longer predictable. The Chairman of the Board of the National Association of Manufacturers provides a vivid account of the crisis.

—USA Today (writer and date unknown)

Like a plague of locusts, U.S. lawyers with their clients have descended upon America and are suing the country out of business. Literally. The number of product liability suits and the size of jury awards are soaring. Filings of personal injury cases in federal courts have jumped 600% in the past decade. Product liability suits filed in federal cases doubled from 1978 to 1985.

—USA Today (writer and date unknown)

In 1974 the average liability jury award was $345,000. Last year it averaged more than $1 million.

—USA Today (writer and date unknown)

Product liability suits have brought a blood bath for U.S. businesses and are distorting our traditional values. We're now the most litigious country on earth—one of every fifteen Americans filed a private civil suit last year. The judicial system is so clogged with cases, delays, continuances, appeals and legal shenanigans that it's slugging its way through a perpetual traffic jam...Americans have developed a mad romance...with the civil litigation process.

—USA Today (writer and date unknown)

[Anne] Strick's book (Injustice for All) offers a comprehensive indictment of the adversarial model, demonstrating that the problems frequently attributed to our legal system are "due less to any venality or inadequacy of the legal professionals than to the intrinsic nature of the adversarial ethic itself." She urges that "consensus through cooperative exploration...replace the concept of truth through battle."

—Alfie Kohn, No Contest

In England, justice is open to all—like the Ritz Hotel.

    —Lord Justice Sir James Mathew

All-gain agreements can only be achieved when the parties stress the co-operative, and not just the competitive, aspects of their relationship.

    —L. Susskind and J. Cruikshank, *Breaking the Impasse*

The good news is that innovative dispute resolution techniques are being used more and more to supplement traditional decision-making processes at all levels of local, state and federal government. Mediation, facilitation and other forms of assisted negotiation have filtered into the legislative, administrative and judicial systems throughout the United States.

    —*Consensus*, Nov. 1988, Harvard Law School Program on Negotiation

Over the next generation, I predict that society's greatest opportunities will lie in tapping human inclinations toward collaboration and compromise rather than stirring our proclivities for competition and rivalry. If lawyers are not leaders in marshaling cooperation and designing mechanisms which allow it to flourish, they will not be at the center of one of the most creative social experiments of our time.

    —Derek Bok, Harvard Law School President

APPENDIX C

PROCLAMATION OF "JUSTICE IS...JUST US"

Proclamation
CONFLICT RESOLUTION DAY OF OTTAWA-CARLETON
September 29, 1988

With a sense that Justice is, ultimately, Just Us, accepting that conflict is universal and an inevitable part of everyone's life, the people wish to be empowered to deal with conflict positively and peacefully;

It being the purpose of the Dispute Resolution Centre of Ottawa-Carleton, with the assistance of the Canadian Institute for Conflict Resolution, both charitable organizations, to explore, promote and implement alternative forms of dispute resolution and to develop life skill programs for individuals to enhance their own abilities to negotiate and mediate their own disputes in their neighbourhood, workplace and everyday lives;

Whereas it is recognized that alternative forms of dispute resolution are meant to supplement not supplant the traditional and institutional processes;

And Whereas the adversarial nature of dispute resolution in any form is becoming increasingly understood as yet still a necessary but only one in a growing range of options that can and should be utilized by individuals and groups to resolve disputes, each having its own advantages and disadvantages so that the people should have the appropriate choices available;

And Whereas it has been observed that non-adversarial processes have been developing at an extraordinary pace, such as conciliation, facilitation, mediation, arbitration, and other hopeful models with room for creating any other effective methods which involve fair, efficient, and affordable alternatives with the assistance of a third party to resolve conflict or settle disputes;

And Whereas the people respect and wish to improve upon and preserve the noble traditions of the legal system;

And Whereas the people believe that the best resolution of a dispute comes, where possible, in promoting "win-win" strategies and adopting attitudes and creating processes to achieve that end, including seeking to discover underlying causes of dispute to avoid needless controversy;

And Whereas the experiences and thinking of all disciplines, different areas of law and various cultures and jurisdictions should be investigated and drawn upon to stimulate "real world" change in the ways that we handle our differences;

And Whereas the public wish, on a community-based footing, to work with all of those involved in the administration of justice in relieving the stress on the courts and to become more educated in these matters;

And Whereas it is recognized that life skills can be learned and applied in everyday situations to mediate disputes;

And Whereas the people wish to encourage our youth and educators in maintaining and expanding life skill techniques such as peer mediation and conflict skills management curriculums and other like programs by raising public awareness of their social contribution and meaning for our times and future generations;

And Whereas the people, sharing a common urge that the world be made safe for diversity, wish to better understand the interrelationship between interpersonal and international conflict;

Now Therefore the Municipalities of Ottawa-Carleton and the Regional Government do hereby proclaim September 29th , 1988 as Conflict Resolution Day of Ottawa-Carleton.

Signed at Ottawa, Ontario, Canada this 28th day of September 1988.

Andrew Haydon,
Chairman, Regional Municipality of Ottawa-Carleton

Harry Allen,
Mayor, City of Gloucester

Des Adam,
Mayor, City of Kanata

Benjamin Franklin,
Mayor, City of Nepean

Gisele Lalonde,
Mayor, City of Vanier

Patrick Murray,
Mayor, Village of Rockcliffe Park

James Durrell,
Mayor, City of Ottawa

Eric Craig,
Mayor, Township of West Carleton

Peter Clark,
Mayor, Township of Cumberland

Anton Wytenburg,
Mayor, Township of Goulbourn

Albert Bouwers,
Mayor, Township of Osgoode

Glenn Brooks,
Mayor, Township of Rideau

APPENDIX D

ALTERNATIVE DISPUTE RESOLUTION—
AN ADR PRIMER

The American Bar Association

Standing Committee on Dispute Resolution Government Affairs and Public Service Groups;
Frank E.A. Sander, Chair; Beth A. Paulson and Larry Ray
1987

This excellent booklet uses the following definition of ADR:

ADR refers to a broad range of mechanisms and processes designed to assist parties in resolving differences. These alternative mechanisms are not intended to supplant court adjudication, but rather to supplement it.

ADR provides an opportunity to resolve conflicts creatively and effectively, finding the process that best handles a particular dispute. It is useful for resolving many disputes that never get to court, as well as providing means of settling 90 to 95 percent of the cases that are filed in court.

The primer describes the following processes: arbitration (private and voluntary; compulsory, non-binding, court-annexed); mediation (rights-based; interest-based, therapeutic); negotiation; private judging; neutral fact finding; ombudsmen; mini-trials; summary jury trials; and the mediated settlement conference (MSC) with a panel of neutral lawyers.

Lawyers are described as advocates and third-party neutrals, who initially help identify the most appropriate processes for the dispute and work ADR techniques into existing law practices.

The content of this primer is presented in the form of succinct answers to common questions that often arise in ADR:

- What is Alternative Dispute Resolution (ADR)?
- What role is there for lawyers in ADR?
- I have heard that ADR is useful for small claims and disputes between neighbors. Does it have anything to do with big commercial litigation?
- In what other types of cases has ADR been employed?
- Won't ADR just add another layer to the already complex judicial system?
- If a lawyer is doing his or her job, why can't the lawyer negotiate a settlement on behalf of his or her client without having to use ADR?
- Won't lawyer-mediators face ethical problems of dual representation or conflict of interest?

- Do people compromise their legal rights or is due process threatened when ADR is used?
- ADR sounds good but what happens if there is a disparity in bargaining power or resources between the disputants? How can the weaker party be protected and not disadvantaged during the settlement process?
- How can ADR proceedings be kept confidential?
- I have heard that lawyers are required to present their entire case during the ADR process. If so, won't this expose both strengths and weaknesses which may be used as a discovery tool by opposing counsel if later the case must go to court?
- Since there are no formal discovery procedures when using ADR, how can I be sure that the other side is not hiding crucial information needed to reach a fair and just settlement?
- I have no opportunity to cross-examine during the ADR process; how can I assess the truthfulness of the opposition's statements?
- How are ADR agreements enforced?
- How do I neutralize any inference of weakness when I propose ADR?
- I am in favor of using ADR. How do I get the other side to participate?
- If I refer a client to a mediator, how can I be sure that the mediator is competent and will skillfully handle the matter?
- I have heard that ADR is disadvantageous to lawyers' financial interests. Is this true?
- What can my firm do to make greater use of ADR?
- What are the fee arrangements for lawyers who either provide ADR, ADR advice or refer clients to ADR practitioners?
- How do I get into the ADR field?
- How can I learn more about ADR?

SOURCES AND REFERENCES

BOOKS

Abella, Rosalie, and Melvin Rothman, eds. *Justice Beyond Orwell*. Montreal: Y. Blais, 1985.

Adler, Mortimer J. *Ten Philosophical Mistakes*. New York: Macmillan, 1985.

Alper, B.S., and L.T. Nichols. *Beyond the Courtroom: Programs in Community Justice and Conflict Resolution*. Lexington, MA: Lexington Books, 1981.

Andrews, C.F. *Mahatma Gandhi's Ideas: Including Selections from His Writings*. 3rd ed. London: George Allen & Unwin Ltd., 1949.

Axelrod, Robert. *The Evolution of Cooperation*. New York: Basic Books, 1984.

Barrett, Jerome T., with Joseph P. Barrett. *A History of Alternative Dispute Resolution: The Story of a Political, Cultural, and Social Movement*. Published in affiliation with the Association for Conflict Resolution. San Francisco: Jossey-Bass, 2004.

Batten, Jack. *Lawyers*. Toronto: Penguin Books, 1985.

Beer, Jennifer E. *Peacemaking in Your Neighborhood: Reflections on an Experiment in Community Mediation*. Philadelphia: New Society Publishers, 1986.

Booth, Mark, ed. *What I Believe: 13 Eminent People of Our Time Argue for Their Philosophy*. New York: Crossroad Publishing, 1984.

Brazil, Wayne D. *Effective Approaches to Settlement: A Handbook for Lawyers and Judges*. Upper Saddle River, NJ: Prentice Hall, 1988.

Browne, Harry. *How I Found Freedom in an Unfree World: A Handbook of Personal Freedom*. New York: MacMillan, 1973.

Buckley, William F. *Overdrive: A Personal Documentary*. New York: Doubleday, 1983.

Cahn, Edmond. *The Moral Decision: Right and Wrong in the Light of American Law*. Bloomington: Indiana University Press, 1956.

Carroll, Lewis. *Through the Looking-Glass*. New York: Mansfield and Wessels, 1899.

Chadman, Charles E., ed. *Cyclopedia of Law*. 12 vols. Chicago: De Bower-Elliott, 1908.

Cleary, Thomas. *The Art of War: Sun Tzu*. Boston: Shambhala Publications, 1988.

Connell, Evan S. *Son of the Morning Star: Custer and The Little Bighorn*. San Francisco: North Point Press, 1984.

CPR Legal Program. *ADR and the Courts: A Manual for Judges and Lawyers*. Erika S. Fine and Elizabeth Plapinger, eds. New York: Butterworth Legal Publishers, 1987.

CPR Legal Program. *Containing Legal Costs: ADR Strategies for Corporations, Law Firms and Government*. Erika S. Fine and Elizabeth Plapinger, eds. New York: Butterworth Legal Publications, 1988.

Dinovas, Anthony J. *World Peace?* Dexter, Michigan: Thomas Shore, Inc., 1984.

Durant, Will. *Caesar and Christ: A History of Roman Civilization and of Christianity from Their Beginnings to A.D. 325.* 11 vols. New York: MJF Books, 1944.

Emond, D. Paul, ed. *Commercial Dispute Resolution: Alternatives to Litigation.* Aurora, Ont.: Canada Law Book, 1989.

Ferencz, Benjamin B. *A Common Sense Guide to World Peace.* New York: Oceana Publications, 1985.

Ferencz, Benjamin B., with Ken Keyes, Jr. *PlanetHood.* New York: Vision Books, 1988

Fischer, Louis. *The Life of Mahatma Gandhi.* New York: Harper & Row, 1950.

Fisher, Roger, and Scott Brown. *Getting Together: Building a Relationship that Gets to Yes.* Boston: Houghton, Mifflin, 1988.

Fisher, Roger, and William Ury. *Getting to Yes.* New York: Penguin Books, 1981.

Fitzpatrick, Peter, and Alan Hunt, eds. *Critical Legal Studies.* Oxford: Basil Blackwell, 1987.

Fromm, Erich. *The Anatomy of Human Destructiveness.* New York: Holt, Rinehart and Winston, 1973.

Galbraith, John Kenneth. *The Age of Uncertainty.* Boston: Houghton Mifflin, 1977.

Goldberg, Stephen B., Eric D. Green, and Frank E.A. Sander. *Dispute Resolution.* Boston: Little, Brown and Co., 1985.

Griffiths, Franklyn, and John C. Polanyi, eds. *The Dangers of Nuclear War: A Pugwash Symposium.* Toronto: University of Toronto Press, 1979.

Harvey, Cameron, Q.C. *Legal Wit and Whimsy: An Anthology of Legal Humour.* Toronto: Carswell, 1988.

Henry, James F., and Jethro K. Lieberman. *The Manager's Guide to Resolving Legal Disputes: Better Results Without Litigation.* New York: Harper & Row, 1985.

Hunter, Ian. *Malcolm Muggeridge: A Life.* London: Collins, 1980.

Hutchinson, Allan C., and Patrick Monahan, eds. *The Rule of Law: Ideal or Ideology.* Toronto: Carswell Legal Publications, 1987.

Hutchinson, Allan C., ed. *Critical Legal Studies.* Lanham, MD: Rowman & Littlefield, 1989.

Jendt, Fred E. *Win-Win Negotiating: Turning Conflict into Agreement.* New York: Wiley and Sons, 1985.

Kilpatrick, Anne Osborne. *Resolving Community Conflict: An Annotated Bibliography.* Athens, GA: University of Georgia, 1983.

Kohn, Alfie. *No Contest: The Case Against Competition.* Boston: Houghton Mifflin, 1986.

Lorenz, Konrad. *On Aggression.* New York: Wolff Books, 1963.

McCormack, Mark H. *What They Don't Teach You at Harvard Business School: Notes from a Street-Smart Executive.* New York: Bantam, 1984.

Moore, Christopher W. *The Mediation Process: Practical Strategies for Resolving Conflict.* San Francisco: Jossey-Bass, 1986.

Mowat, R.C. *Climax of History.* London: Blandford Press, 1951.

Muller, Robert. *A Planet of Hope.* New York: Amity House, 1985.

Ouspensky, P.D. *A New Model of the Universe.* London: Kegan Paul, 1931.

Paine, Thomas. *Common Sense*. 1776.

Peck, M. Scott. *The Different Drum—Community Making and Peace*. New York: Simon & Schuster, 1987.

Peters, Thomas J., and Robert H. Waterman, Jr. *In Search of Excellence: Lessons from America's Best-Run Companies*. New York: Harper & Row, 1982.

Provine, D. Marie. *Settlement Strategies for Federal District Judges*. Washington, D.C: Federal Judicial Center, 1985.

Reader's Digest Association. *You and the Law: A Practical Guide to Canadian Law*. Third edition. Toronto: Reader's Digest, 1984.

Sandole, Dennis J., and Ingrid Sandole-Staroste, eds. *Conflict Management and Problem Solving: Interpersonal to International Affairs.*. London: Francis Pinter, 1987.

Schud, Edwin M. *Law and Society—A Social View*. NP: Colonial Press, 1969.

Snow, C.P. *Variety of Men*. New York: Scribner, 1966.

Strick, Anne. *Injustice for All: How our Adversary System of Law Victimizes Us and Subverts True Justice*. New York: Penguin, 1978.

Susskind, Lawrence, and Jeffrey Cruikshank. *Breaking the Impasse: Consensual Approaches to Resolving Public Disputes*. New York: Basic Books Inc., 1987.

Ury, William, Jeanne Brette, and Stephen Goldberg. *Getting Disputes Resolved: Designing Systems to Cut the Costs of Conflict*. San Francisco: Jossey-Bass, 1988.

Warner, Ralph, and Toni Phara. *29 Reasons Not to Go to Law School*. Berkeley: Nolo Press, 1982.

Watch Tower Bible and Tract Society of Pennsylvania. *An Aid to Bible Understanding*. Brooklyn: Watch Tower Bible and Tract Society of Pennsylvania, 1971.

White, D. Robert. *The Official Lawyer's Handbook*. New York: Simon & Schuster, 1983.

JOURNALS AND PERIODICALS

Arthurs, H.W. "Alternatives to the Formal Justice System: Reminiscing About the Future." *Cost* 1.

Bazda, E.D. "The Process of Dispute Resolution." *Beyond Orwell* 193 (1985).

Burger, Chief Justice Warren E. "Isn't There a Better Way? Annual Report on the State of the Judiciary." *ABA Journal* 68 (1982).

Bok, Derek. "Law and Its Discontents: A Critical Look at Our Legal System." *Bar Leader* (March–April 1983).

Bowlby, J.D. "Conference on the Cost of Justice." *Canadian Legal Aid Bill* 4 (1981).

Brazil, Wayne D. "Special Master in Complex Cases: Extending the Judiciary of Reshaping Adjudication." *University of Chicago Law Review* 53 (1986).

Brooks. "The Judge and the Adversary System." *The Canadian Judiciary* (1976).

Bush. "Dispute Resolution: Alternatives and Achieving the Goals of Civil Justice: Jurisdictional Principles for Process Choice." *Wisconsin Law Review* (1984).

Cain, Maureen, and Kalman Kulcsar. "Thinking Disputes: An Essay on the Origins of the Dispute Industry." *Law and Society Review* 16 (1981–1982).

Calabresi, G. "Too Much, Too Little, or Both: Some Thoughts on Law Making in American Courts." *Cambridge Lecture* 1 (1983).

Cappelletti, M., and B. Garth. "Access to Justice as a Focus of Research." *Windsor Yearbook of Access to Justice* 1 (1981).

Condlin, Robert J. "Cases on Both Sides: Patterns of Argument in Legal Dispute Negotiations." *Maryland Law Review* 44: 65.

Downes, T.A., et al. "The Future of Legal Services in Britain: A client or lawyer oriented approach." *Windsor Yearbook of Access to Justice* 1 (1981): 121.

Edelman, Peter B. "Institutionalizing Dispute Resolution Alternatives." *The Justice System Journal* 9 (1984): 134.

Edwards, Harry T. "Alternative Dispute Resolution: Panacea or Anathema?" *Harvard Law Review* 99 (1986): 688.

Eisenberg, Melvin Aron. "Private Ordering Through Negotiation Dispute—Settlement and Rule Making." *Harvard Law Review* 89 (1976): 637.

———. "Negotiation Dispute—Settlement and Rule Making." *Harvard Law Review* 89 (1976):4.

Elliott, E. Donald. "Managerial Judging and the Evolution of Procedure." *University of Chicago Law Review* 53 (1986): 306.

Felstiner, William L.F., Richard Abel, and Austen Sarat. "The Emergence and Transformation of Disputes: Naming, Blaming, Claiming." *Law and Society Review* 15 (1980–1981): 652.

Estey, W.Z. "Who Needs Courts?" *Windsor Yearbook of Access to Justice* 1 (1981): 263.

———. "The Changing Role of the Judiciary." *Cambridge Lecture* (1983): 329.

Fiss, Owen M. "Against Settlement." *The Yale Law Journal* 93 (1984).

———. "Out of Eden." *The Yale Law Journal* 94 (1985).

Fuller, Lon L. "The Forms and Limits of Adjudication." *Harvard Law Review* 92 (1978).

Galanter, Marc. "The Day After the Litigation Explosion." *Maryland Law Review* 46 (1986).

Gifford, Donald G. "A Context-Based Theory of Strategy Selection in Legal Negotiations." *Ohio State Law Journal* 46 (1985).

Gnaizda, Robert. "Secret Justice for the Privileged Few." *Judicature* 66 (June–July 1982).

Gulliver, P.H. "Negotiations as a Model of Dispute, Settlement Towards a General Model." *Law Society Review* (Summer 1973).

Horrocks, R.L. "Alternatives to the Courts in Canada." *Alberta Law Review* 20 (1982).

Howland, W.G.C. "Is the Face of the Justice Changing?" *Gazette* 15 (1981).

Hutchinson, Allan C. "The Formal and Informal Schemes of the Civil Justice System: A Legal Symbiosis Explored." *Osgoode Hall Law Journal* 19 (1981).

Iacano, P.M. "Alternative Dispute Resolution." *Advocates' Society Journal* 5 (1986).

Jordan, Ellen R. "Should Litigants Have a Choice Between Specialized Courts and Courts of General Jurisdiction?" *Judicature* 66 (June–July 1982).

Kidder, Robert L. "The End of the Road? Problems in the Analysis of Disputes." *Law and Society Review* 15 (1980–1981).

Kohn, Alfie. "It's Hard to Get Left Out of a Pair." *Psychology Today*, October 1987.

Kritzer, Herbert M. "The Judge's Role in Pre-Trial Case Procedure: Assessing the Need for Change." *Judicature* 66 (June–July 1982).

Lafontaine, Y. "Are Lawyers a Vivid Contradiction?" *Cynical Society* (1985).

Laue, James H., Sharon Burde, William Potapchuk, and Miranda Salkoff. "Getting to the Table: Three Paths." *Mediation Quarterly* 20 (1988).

Levy, H.J. "Changes Uncertain, but Certainly Change." *Canadian Lawyer* 4 (1978).

Lieberman, Jethro K., and James F. Henry. "Lessons from the Alternative Dispute Movement." *University of Chicago Law Review* 53 (1986).

Lightman, J., and M.J. Missman. "Salary or Fee for Service in Delivering Legal Aid Services: Theory and Practice in Canada." *Queen's Law Journal* 10 (1984).

Linden, Mr. Justice Allen M. "In Praise of Settlement: The Need for Cooperation." *Canadian Community Law Journal* 7 (1984).

MacDonald, R.A. "Speedy Justice for the Litigant: Sound Jurisprudence for the Province." *Osgoode Hall Law Review* 16, no. 3 (1978).

Marshall, James. "Lawyers, Truth and Zero-Sum Game." *Notre Dame Lawyer* 47.

McEwen, Craig A. "Differing Visions of Alternative Dispute Resolution and Formal Law." *The Justice System Journal* 12 (1987).

McGovern, Francis E. "Toward a Functional Approach for Managing Complex Litigation." *University of Chicago Law Review* 53 (1986).

McMurtry, R.R. "Roy's the Name, Tightrope's the Game." *Canadian Lawyer* 2, no. 4 (1978).

McThenia, Andrew M., and Thomas L. Shaffer. "For Reconciliation." *The Yale Law Journal* 94 (1985).

Megarry, J. "Justice: Different Perspectives." *Provincial Judges Journal* 7 (1983).

Menkel-Meadow, Carrie. "Toward Another View of Legal Negotiations: The Structure of Problem-Solving." *UCLA Law Review* 31 (1984).

———. "For and Against Settlement: Uses and Abuses of the Mandatory Settlement Conference." *UCLA Law Review* 33 (1985).

Merry, Sally. "Dispute Resolution by Goldberg, Green and Sander." *Harvard Law Review* 100 (1987).

Merry, Sally, and Susan S. Sibley. "What do Plaintiffs Want? Re-examining the Concept of Dispute." *The Justice System Journal* 9 (1984).

Nader, Laura. "Disputing Without the Force of Law." *The Yale Law Journal* 88 (1979).

Nadon, J. "Commercial Courts." *National Creditor Review* 83 (1986).

Newman, John O. "Rethinking Fairness Perspectives in the Litigation Process." *The Yale Law Journal* 94 (1985).

Palmer, J. "The Growing Irrelevance of the Civil Courts." *Windsor Yearbook of Access to Justice* 5 (1985).

Parker, W.D. "A History of the Common Law and the Adversarial System in Canada." *Advocates' Society Journal* 5 (1986).

Pipkin, Ronald M., and Janet Rifkin. "The Social Organization in Alternative Dispute Resolution: Implications for Professionalization of Mediation." *The Justice System Journal* 9 (1984).

Perritt, Henry H., Jr. "And the Whole World Was of One Language: A Broad View of Dispute Resolution." *Villanova Law Review* 29 (1983–1984).

Pirie, Andrew J. "The Lawyer as Mediator: Professional Responsibility Problems or Professional Problems?" *Canadian Bar Review* 63 (1985).

Posner, Richard J. "The Summary Jury Trial and Other Methods of Alternative Dispute Resolution: Some Cautionary Observations." *The University of Chicago Law Review* 53 (1986).

Pruitt, Dean G. "Solutions Not Winners." *Psychology Today*, December 1987.

Rabow, Gerald. "The Co-operative Edge." *Psychology Today*, January 1988.

Rappaport, A. "Public Policy and the Dilemma of Diversion." *Current Issues* (1983).

Resnick, Judith. "Failing Faith: Adjudicatory Procedure in Decline." *The University of Chicago Law Review* 53 (1986).

———. "Managerial Judges." *Harvard Law Review* 96 (1982).

Riskin, Leonard. "Toward New Standards for the Neutral Lawyer in Mediation." *Arizona Law Review* 26 (1984).

———. "Mediation and Lawyers." *Ohio State Law Journal* 43 (1982).

Robinette, J.J. "The Prospects for Justice." *Beyond Orwell* (1985).

Rose, I. Nelson. "Litigator's Fallacy." *Whittier Law Review* 6 (1984).

Russell, P.H., and G.D. Watson. "A Quiet Revolution in the Administration of Justice." *Gazette* II (1977).

Sarat, Austen. "The New Formalism in Disputing and Dispute Processing." *Law and Society Review* 21 (1988).

Schlossberg, Nancy K. "Taking the Mystery out of Change." *Psychology Today*, May 1987.

Schuck, Peter H. "The Role of Judges in Settling Complex Cases: The Agent Orange Example." *University of Chicago Law Review* 53 (1986).

Scott, I. "Working Towards Access to Justice in Ontario." *Advocates' Society Journal* 5 (1985).

Selva, Lance H., and Robert M. Bohm. "A Critical Examination of the Informalism Experiment in the Administration of Justice." *Civil and Social Justice* 29 (1987).

Socks, Howard R. "Alternative Dispute Resolution Movement: Wave of the Future or Flash in the Pan?" *Alberta Law Review* XXVI, no. 2.

Shetreet, Dr. Simon. "The Administration of Justice: Practical Problems, Value Conflicts and Changing Concepts." *UBC Law Review 13*, no. 1 (1979): 53.

———. "Remedies for Court Congestion and Delay: The Models and the Recent Trend." *University of Western Ontario Law Review* 17 (1979).

———. "The Limits of Expeditious Justice." *Expeditious Justice* (1979).

Simon, William H. "The Ideology of Advocacy: Procedural Justice and Professional Ethics." *Wisconsin Law Review* 29 (1978).

Southin, Mary F., Q.C. "Reflections on Chaos in the Courts." *Advocate* 41 (1983).

Templeton, Sir Sydney. "The Law and Lawyers in the 80's." *Manitoba Law Journal* (1981).

Thompson, Bonita. "Resolving Business Conflict." *Canadian Banker* (May–June 1988).

Thomson, M.N. "Dispute Resolution in Japan: The Non-Litigation." *Advocate* 43 (1985).

Tomasic, Roman. "Mediation as an Alternative: Rhetoric and Reality in the Neighborhood Justice Movement." In *Neighborhood Justice: Assessment of an Emerging Idea*, edited by Roman Tomasic and Malcolm M. Feeley. New York: Longman, 1982.

Trubec, David M. "The Construction and Deconstruction of a Disputes-Focused Approach: An Afterward." *Law and Society Review* 15 (1980–1981).

Schwartz, Murray L. "The Professionalism and Accountability of Lawyers." *California Law Review* 66 (1978).

Stradiotto, Rene A. "The Advocates Society." *Q.C. Journal* 7, No. 4. Special Issue, Michaelmas Term (August 1988).

Walker, William Laurens, and John W. Thibault. "An Experimental Examination of Pre-Trial Conference Techniques." *Minnesota Law Review* 55 (1971).

Walker, M.C. "Congestion and Delay in the Provincial Court (Criminal Division)." *University of Toronto Faculty of Law Review* 82 (1984).

Weckstein, Donald T. "The Purposes of Dispute Resolution: Comparative Concepts of Justice." *American Business Law Journal* 26 (1988).

Weiler, P. "The Canadian Judicial System: The Criminal and Civil Processes." *Law and Politics* 56 (1984).

Zemans. Frederick H. "Recent Trends in the Organization of Legal Services." *Queens Law Journal* 26 (1985).

[Author unknown.] "The California Rent-A-Judge Experiment: Constitutional and Policy Considerations of Pay-As-You-Go Courts." *Harvard Law Review* 94 (1981): 1593.

[Author unknown.] "Alternative Dispute Resolution: Meeting the Legal Needs of the 1980's." *Ohio State Journal* 1, No. 1 (1985).

[Author unknown.] "Symposium: Alternative Dispute Resolution in Canada–U.S. Trade Relations." *Maine Law Review* 40, No. 2 (1988).

WORKING PAPERS AND OTHER UNPUBLISHED WORKS

Bailey, Martha. "A Feminist Critique of the Family Mediation Movement." Master's thesis, Queen's University, Faculty of Law, 1988.

Community Board Program. "Prospectus." Working Paper Series #7. San Francisco.

Conflict Resolution Network of Australia. "Fighting Fair: A Guide."

Dispute Processing Research Program, Institute for Legal Studies, University of Wisconsin, Madison Law School, Working Papers series:

Bash, Robert A. Baruch. "Defining Quality in Dispute Resolution Taxonomies and Anti-Taxonomies of Process, Contexts, Interests and Standards." Series #8-7.

Bilder, Richard. "International Dispute Settlement and the Role of Adjudication." Series #7-8.

Esser, John. "The State of the Art in ADR Evaluation: We Don't Know What We Think and We Don't Think What We Know." Series #8-10.

Galanter, Marc. "The Day After the Litigation Explosion." Series #7-9.

Kritzner, Herbert M. "The Form of Negotiation in Ordinary Litigation." Series #7-2.

————. "The Lawyer as Negotiator: Working in the Shadows." Series #7-4.

————. "Political Culture and the Propensity to Sue." Series #9-1.

RuBino, Richard G., and Harvey M. Jacobs. "Predicting the Utility of Environmental Mediation: Natural Resource and Conflict Typologies as a Guide to Environment Conflict Assessment." Series #9-3.

Selby, Susan, and Austen Sarat. "Dispute Processing in Law and Legal Scholarship: From Institutional Critique to the Reconstitution of the Judicial Subject." Series #8-9.

Tyler, Tom. "The Quality of Dispute Resolution Process and Outcomes: Measurement Problems and Possibilities." Series #8-8.

National Associations Active in Criminal Justice. "A Reflective Analysis in Reconciliation as it Relates to Criminal Justice: A Search for Community-Building Justice." Discussion paper prepared for the New Divisions of Criminal Justice workshop, Ottawa, Ontario, May 6–7, 1987.

Ontario Law Reform Commission. "Alternative Dispute Resolution Program Proposal." December 9, 1987.

CONFERENCE PAPERS AND MATERIALS

American Bar Association. "Mediation and Education: Exploring the Alternatives." A workshop of the Standing Committee on Dispute Resolution. April 8–10, 1988.

American Bar Association. 110th Annual Conference. "ADR: Is it For Real?" Workshop session of the Torts and Insurance Practice Session, Alternative Dispute Resolution Committee. Toronto, Ontario, August 10, 1988.

Association Internationale des Jeunes Avocats. "International Arbitration Commission Working Session on Alternative Methods of Dispute Settlement." September 7, 1988, Munich, Germany.

Canadian Bar Association, Ontario Continuing Legal Education. "Alternative Dispute Resolution: What's All the Fuss About and Where is it Going?" Toronto, Ontario, October 3, 1988.

David, Jenny. "Are Lawyers Becoming Obsolete as Dispute Resolvers?" Paper delivered at the 43rd annual conference of the Australian Universities Law School Association. August 30, 1988.

Linden, Mr. Justice Allen. "Dispute Resolution in Canada." Paper delivered at a meeting of the Special Committee on Dispute Resolution, American Bar Association. San Diego, California, January 30–31, 1987.

Ministry of the Attorney General of Ontario. "Conference on Access to Civil Justice." June 20–22, 1988. Toronto, Ontario.

REPORTS

American Bar Association Standing Committee on Dispute Resolution, Public Service Division. *Multi-Door Court House Experience: An Innovative Expansion of Justice.*

Canadian Bar Association. *Ontario ADR Committee, First Report.* May 24, 1988.

Church Council on Justice and Corrections. *Consultation on the Report of the Canadian Sentencing Commission.* Cosponsored by the federal Department of Justice. June 2–3, 1988.

Endispute, Inc. *Making Alternative Dispute Resolution Work: An Endispute Guide for Practicing Lawyers and Business People.* Chicago: 1987.

National Associations Active in Criminal Justice. *A Reflective Analysis in Reconciliation as it Relates to Criminal Justice.* Proceedings of a workshop. May 6–7, 1987.

National Associations Active in Criminal Justice. *The Purpose of Criminal Law: Towards a Social Responsibility Model of Criminal Justice.* Proceedings of the NAACJ Seminar. December 1987.

Pirie, Andrew J. *Dispute Resolution in Canada: Present State, Future Direction.* Report of the Law Reform Commission of Canada. April 1987.

Pitsula, Pat. *Report on Alternative Dispute Resolution Projects.* Burnaby, B.C.: Simon Fraser University, 1987.

Province of British Columbia. *Access to Justice.* Report of the Justice Reform Committee. November 1988.

Standing Committee on Justice and Solicitor-General. *Taking Responsibility.* Report of the Standing Committee on Justice and Solicitor-General on its Review of Sentencing, Conditional Release and Related Aspects of Correction. David Daubney, M.P., Chairman. August 1988.

The Connecticut ADR Project, Inc. Final Report. 1988.

Victoria Mediation Arbitration Centre. *Alternative Dispute Resolution for Minor Civil Disputes*: Submission to the Justice Reform Commission.

Zuber, The Honourable T.G. *Report of the Ontario Courts Inquiry.* Toronto: Queen's Printer for Ontario, 1987.

NEWSLETTERS AND OTHER PUBLICATIONS

"Alternative to Judicial Dispute Resolution." Supplement to *Los Angeles Daily Journal* and *San Francisco Daily Journal*, Sept. 2, 1988.

"The Legal Practice Report." *Of Counsel,* Vol.7, No.4. Feb. 15, 1988.

Australian Alternative to Judicial Dispute Resolution.

Australian Commercial Disputes Centre. *Resolution of Commercial Disputes.*

British Columbia International Commercial Arbitration Centre. *Arbitration in Canada.* Vancouver.

Center for Public Resources. *Alternatives.* New York.

National Association of Mediation in Education. *The Fourth R.* Michigan, U.S.

National Institute for Dispute Resolution. *Dispute Resolution Forum..*

Network for Community Justice and Conflict Resolution. *Community Justice Report.* Kitchener, Ontario.

The Church Council on Justice and Corrections. *Update.*

The Public Disputes Network. *Consensus.* Harvard Law School, Program on Negotiation.